MODERN
MEDITERRANEAN

To my late father; thank you for your constant encouragement and support throughout my career. To Jessica, Bruno & Gabriela; may you learn to love food as much as I do and may all your meals be happy ones with love and laughter.

Modern Mediterranean
Marc Fosh

First published in the UK and USA in 2019 by Nourish, an imprint of Watkins Media Limited
Unit 11, Shepperton House, 83–93 Shepperton Road
London N1 3DF

enquiries@nourishbooks.com

Commissioning Editor: Kate Fox
Managing Editor: Daniel Hurst
Head of Design: Georgina Hewitt
Production: Uzma Taj
Copy Editor: Emily Preece-Morrison
Commissioned Photography: Nando Esteva

A CIP record for this book is available from the British Library

ISBN: 978-1-848993-70-9

10 9 8 7 6 5 4 3 2 1

Typeset in Walbaum
Colour reproduction by XY Digital
Printed in China

Publisher's note
While every care has been taken in compiling the recipes for this book, Watkins Media Limited, or any other persons who have been involved in working on this publication, cannot accept responsibility for any errors or omissions, inadvertent or not, that may be found in the recipes or text, nor for any problems that may arise as a result of preparing one of these recipes. If you are pregnant or breastfeeding or have any special dietary requirements or medical conditions, it is advisable to consult a medical professional before following any of the recipes contained in this book.

Notes on the recipes
Unless otherwise stated:
Use medium fruit and vegetables
Use medium (US large) organic or free-range eggs
Use fresh herbs, spices and chillies
Use granulated sugar (Americans can use ordinary granulated sugar when caster sugar is specified)
Do not mix metric, imperial and US cup measurements:
1 tsp = 5ml 1 tbsp = 15ml 1 cup = 240ml

nourishbooks.com

Marc Fosh

MODERN
MEDITERRANEAN

NOURISH

EAT WELL, LIVE WELL

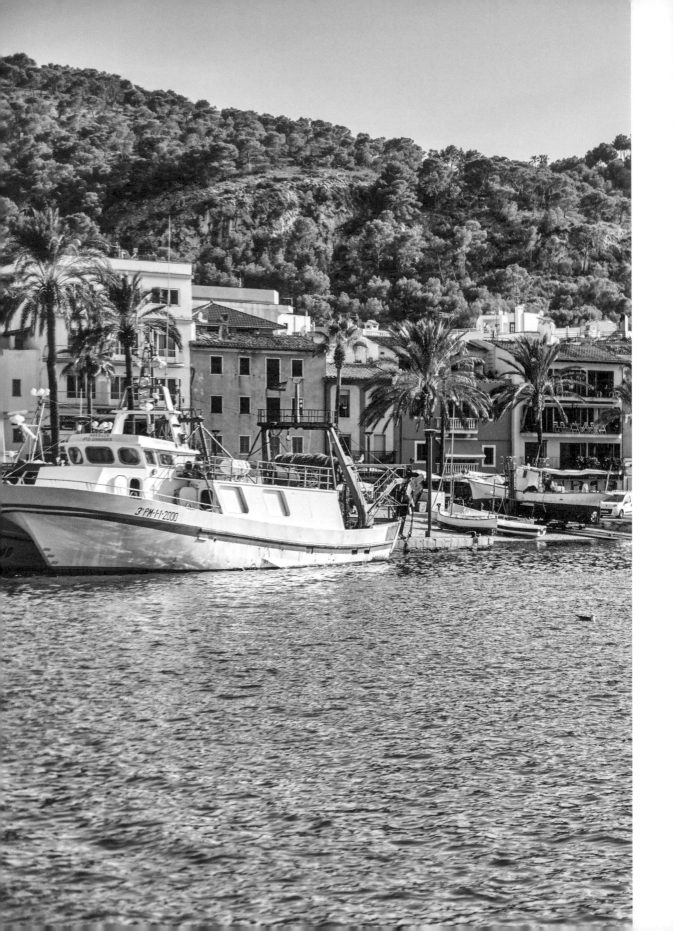

INTRODUCTION

IN SEARCH OF SUNSHINE

I first came to live and work in Mallorca almost twenty-five years ago. I received my chef's training in London and cut my teeth in the city's Michelin-starred restaurants, which – at that time – had a focus on traditional, French techniques with a reliance on cream and butter. Searching for a little sunshine and a lighter approach to cooking, I then spent three wonderful years cheffing my way around the Basque city of San Sebastián – the food capital of Spain – before finally arriving in Mallorca with a new passion for the food and produce of the Mediterranean and a thirst to learn more. Compared to the culinary mecca of San Sebastián, the gastronomic scene in Mallorca was much more sedate, but the island's unique climate meant that the local produce was spectacular. I immediately knew that this would be a wonderful place to open a restaurant.

Before coming to Mallorca, I had no idea how beautiful and diverse the island actually is. When you fly over it for the first time, you soon realise that the island is very green, with wonderful mountain ranges and some of the most stunning coastline of the Mediterranean. Driving around, the incredibly beautiful scenery is filled with almond, olive and orange groves. I very quickly fell in love.

The regional cuisine of Mallorca has its roots firmly planted in the rustic, peasant traditions of the Mediterranean, with a few Arab and Moorish influences thrown in for good measure. At first glance, there doesn't seem to be too much choice, but scratch the surface just a little and you'll find that Mallorcan food is rich and varied, with some surprising flavour combinations and many interesting dishes steeped in tradition and rooted in local ingredients. Long before the arrival of tourism, fishing and farming were absolutely essential for survival on this small, Mediterranean island far from the Spanish mainland; as a result, Mallorca is bursting with amazing seasonal ingredients from its wonderful climate and rich, fertile soil.

Since those early days, Mallorca's gastronomic landscape has changed immeasurably, and it now has a very exciting and dynamic restaurant scene all over the island, where talented young

MODERN MEDITERRANEAN FOOD

It's probably fair to say that, here in the Balearics, although we have always relied heavily on local produce, we took it for granted, and we certainly didn't know how to effectively sell the story of our great cooks, suppliers and producers to the outside world. When you sit down in a restaurant like ours, you will find that our organic olive oil is from my friend Pep Solivellas in the village of Pollença, and the sea salt (flor de sal) is from just along the coastline in Es Trenc. Our menu is littered with local ingredients: Soller prawns, young almonds, sea fennel, samphire, truffles and wild mushrooms from the mountains, fresh fish from the Mediterranean sea, and tender lamb and suckling pig from the surrounding fields. Add the fact that at least sixty per cent of the wines on our list are procured from the island's bodegas and made from indigenous grape varieties by small, passionate wine producers, and you start to realise that Mallorca has an amazing array of fabulous produce right on its doorstep.

chefs are cooking Mediterranean food with local ingredients and great flavours. These are the type of restaurants where you can really feel the passion and individual philosophies of each chef, and I'm proud to say that many of those young chefs have – at some point – passed through my kitchens along the way. The island's traditional farming and agriculture system has also changed, with a wave of small producers making wonderful, artisan ingredients and local markets boasting a wide range of fantastic, locally grown foods to inspire us. Mallorca has finally become a true gastronomic destination.

Recently, the British newspaper the *Telegraph* asked, "Is Mallorca Europe's best island for foodies?" I truly believe that it can be, and that we have only just started to tell our story as we write the next chapter of this beautiful island's culinary history. Mallorca's food revolution is now in full flow – we have a group of innovative chefs who cook with good, local, organic and seasonal produce, who reinvent traditional, Mediterranean recipes with a modern touch while keeping alive the colours, freshness, flavours and textures of the region. We are building on the rich history, heritage and traditions of the Mediterranean and turning them into something new.

KM.0

At restaurant Marc Fosh, we are strong defenders of the cultural values that are transmitted through the local gastronomy. We serve tasting menus that highlight the best local produce we can source from across the Balearic Islands, with ideas and inspiration from all over the Mediterranean. The menus are based on a simple philosophy: food tastes best when it's made from local, seasonal ingredients. Only when you understand and respect the essence of an ingredient can you properly come to enhance its flavour through cooking. Guided by nature, our kitchen reflects the seasons and some of the ingredients are grown on our own farm.

We strongly support local produce and admire the values of the Slow Food movement, which defends responsible consumption, organic farming, seasonal foods, avoiding the use of genetically modified products, and the use of local ingredients within a 100-kilometre radius. This is known as "Km.0", and it's pretty hot right now. The goal is basically to limit the human impact on the environment – less flying, driving and fuel consumption, to leave a smaller eco-footprint. By using farm-fresh produce, we know that it is packed with nutrients and generally doesn't have to be sprayed with chemicals to protect it for a long haul to the restaurant kitchen. Thinking globally and sourcing locally is not just politically correct, it's also personally rewarding

for the farmer, the chef and the diner. Everybody wins. At the end of the day, we are completely reliant on the great, local produce from our suppliers, and without them we would be lost.

MODERN MEDITERRANEAN AT HOME

Keep it fresh, keep it seasonal and make it easy.

This book invites you to recreate the flavours of the Mediterranean using eighteen of my favourite ingredients as a starting point. The ingredients are listed and arranged alphabetically, with a chapter on each food, so you may find both sweet and savoury recipes in each section. The ingredients are there to inspire you to cook fresh, seasonal food that any home cook will be able to prepare easily.

Buying good ingredients is the important first step of any recipe, and

for this I recommend shopping at your local market. Visiting a bustling market is always fun and a feast for the eyes. I love walking around the corner from the restaurant to the Mercat de l'Olivar in Palma – it's where the local residents and chefs come to buy their food and I enjoy the smells and admire how beautifully the vendors display their produce, from the hanging hams and cured sausages to the intricately stacked fruit and vegetables. My favourite is probably the fish section: every day it is packed with fantastically fresh fish and seafood, and it never ceases to inspire me, no matter how many times I visit. A good, fresh, seasonal ingredient – simply cooked – is much more inviting for guests, whether you are cooking in a restaurant for Michelin stars or for family and friends at home. Buying from your local market allows you to support the local agriculture and means that you will eat seasonal, fresh and ripe ingredients throughout the year. This is also a great way to improve your health, but I'm convinced that locally grown foods simply taste better.

Like so many busy people, when I'm cooking at home I don't really want to

spend hours slaving over complicated recipes. My philosophy on cooking for friends and family is to keep it simple, fresh and Mediterranean. Above all, I want it to be the type of food that draws people together, to sit around a table sharing food, wine and conversation. Food is, after all, a communal experience – for all of us in the Mediterranean, it's one of the biggest pleasures in life. Many of the recipes in this book are easy, one-pot dishes that you can bring straight to the table; some are a little more sophisticated, for that special occasion when you want to impress; but all the recipes are quite simple to prepare and cook using ingredients that are readily available in most supermarkets.

When you are planning to cook for friends or family at home, you can make your life so much easier by preparing and organising as much as possible in advance.

Don't worry about ruining a recipe by replacing one ingredient or omitting another; quite often the best recipes are created by trial and error. Remember that a recipe has no soul. You, the cook, must bring soul to the recipe. If there is no passion behind it, the chances are you'll be disappointed. Cooking at home shouldn't be a chore – it should be fun. Most of all, it should be a way of releasing your creative talents, relieving stress and tantalising your taste buds.

I hope that these recipes bring a little warm, Mediterranean sunshine into your kitchen, that they will inspire you, and that you will find cooking them at home to be the wonderful, relaxing experience it's supposed to be. Happy cooking!

Marc

ALMENDRAS

Spain is the world's second largest producer of almonds, and they grow all over the Spanish Mediterranean regions of Catalonia, Valencia, Murcia, Andalusia, Aragón and all over the Balearic Islands. Traditionally, during the harvest in September, the branches of helpless almond trees were beaten by hand with long sticks to release the fruit, which would drop into waiting nets below, but this method is fast disappearing. It's hardly surprising. I tried it myself several years ago and it is unbearably hard, back-breaking work that almost put me off almonds for life. Today, you're more likely to hear the dreadful drone of mechanical tree-shakers as they violently grip and shake the trees into submission.

Almonds have been cultivated since ancient times and are often mentioned in The Bible, although their exact origins are obscure. Unlike oranges, which have to be watered regularly, the almond tree is extremely undemanding. It gets the moisture it requires through its roots, which extend deep into the ground. Spanish almonds are generally of outstanding quality because most of the cultivation takes place on small, dry-farmed orchards. Although these are less productive than extensive, irrigated orchards, the almonds have a higher oil content, which makes them moist and more flavoursome.

Almonds belong to the same family as cherries, apricots and peaches. The delicately flavoured nuts are used throughout the world in both sweet and savoury dishes, and they are often paired with chocolate, apples, pears, strawberries, apricots and fresh figs. The Spanish have invented hundreds of recipes for almonds and they appear in all manner of sweet pastries and cookies, including the famous *turrón* (nougat) and *gato*, an almond sponge cake. They are often used to thicken soups and sauces and form the base *of ajo blanco malagueño*, a refreshing chilled almond and garlic soup from Andalusia.

A recent study showed that almonds can boost the health of people with high cholesterol levels, as most of the fat contained in them is mono-unsaturated, the same type found in olive oil. They are low in carbohydrates, high in vitamin E and a good source of protein. However, experts have been reluctant to recommend nuts to individuals who need to diet because of their high calorie content. Used in moderate amounts, however providing the nuts are natural, without added salt and oils, they can be very healthy and nutritionally valuable foods.

MALLORCAN TURKEY STEW *with* ALMONDS

Cooking time: 25 minutes,
plus standing
Preparation time: 20 minutes
Serves 4

150ml/5fl oz/⅔ cup olive oil
1 skinless turkey breast, diced
1 onion (preferably Spanish),
    finely sliced
2 garlic cloves, crushed
1 tbsp chopped oregano
2 bay leaves
200ml/7fl oz/scant 1 cup dry
    white wine
150ml/5fl oz/⅔ cup dry sherry
300ml/10½fl oz/1¼ cups chicken
    stock (bouillon)
1kg/2lb 3oz potatoes, peeled and
    diced
50g/1¾oz/scant ½ cup toasted
    almonds
2 slices stale white bread
1 tbsp chopped flat-leaf parsley
sea salt and freshly ground black
    pepper

Heat the olive oil in a heavy saucepan over a medium heat and fry the diced turkey breast until it starts to colour. Add the onions, garlic, oregano and bay leaves and fry for 3–4 minutes until the onions are golden brown. Add the white wine, dry sherry and chicken stock (bouillon) and bring to the boil. Add the potatoes, season with salt and pepper, then turn the heat down and gently simmer for 20 minutes.

In a pestle and mortar or food processor, crush the toasted almonds and stale bread to a coarse mixture. Remove the stew from the heat, sprinkle over the almond mixture, then cover with a lid and let stand for 6–8 minutes. Sprinkle with chopped parsley and serve.

CHILLED ALMOND *and* GARLIC SOUP *with* MARINATED SARDINES *and* CHERRIES

Cooking time: 35–40 minutes
Preparation time: 25 minutes, plus chilling
Serves 4

180g/6½oz/1¼ cups peeled almonds
3 garlic cloves, peeled
600ml/21fl oz/2½ cups milk
250ml/9fl oz/1 cup water
50g/1¾oz fresh white bread
2 tbsp sherry vinegar
150ml/5fl oz/⅔ cup olive oil
12 fresh cherries, pitted and halved, to garnish
sea salt and freshly ground black pepper

--- **FOR THE MARINATED SARDINES:**
12 sardines, cleaned and filleted
200g/7oz/¾ cup sea salt
200g/7oz/1 cup caster (superfine) sugar
200ml/7fl oz/scant 1 cup olive oil

Ajo blanco is a breeze to make and keeps well for 2–3 days in the refrigerator. Sometimes known as gazpacho blanco (white gazpacho), the origins actually predate gazpacho by several centuries and date back to the invasion of the Moors, who we also have to thank for our abundance of almonds here in Mallorca.

First, make the marinated sardines. Place the sardine fillets skin-side up on a large dish. Thoroughly combine the salt and sugar and completely cover the sardine fillets with the mixture. Transfer to the refrigerator to marinate for 1–2 hours.

Rinse the marinated sardines in cold water to remove all the salt, then dry with paper towels. Transfer to a clean bowl, cover with olive oil and chill until required.

Meanwhile, in a heavy saucepan, combine the peeled almonds, garlic cloves, milk and water, and cook over a low heat for 30–35 minutes, until the almonds are soft and cooked through. Add the bread and cook for another 3–4 minutes. Remove from the heat and let cool a little, then transfer to a food processor, add the sherry vinegar and blend to a purée. Whisk in the olive oil, season to taste, then pass through a fine sieve (strainer) into a bowl. Chill in the refrigerator for at least 3–4 hours.

To serve, pour the chilled *ajo blanco* into soup bowls and garnish with the marinated sardines and fresh cherries. Serve immediately.

MENJAR BLANC *with* ROSEWATER, RASPBERRY *and* POMEGRANATE SYRUP

Cooking time: 15–20 minutes
Preparation time: 10 minutes, plus chilling
Serves 4

800ml/28fl oz/scant 3½ cups milk
200g/7 oz/1½ cups almonds, peeled and chopped
1 vanilla pod, split
50g/1¾oz/½ cup cornflour (cornstarch)
225g/8oz/scant 1¼ cups cups caster (superfine) sugar
1 cinnamon stick
grated zest of 1 lemon
fresh mint leaves, to garnish

--- **FOR THE ROSEWATER, RASPBERRY AND POMEGRANATE SYRUP:**
120ml/4fl oz/½ cup water
1 tbsp pomegranate molasses
60g/2oz/scant ⅓ cup caster (superfine) sugar
4 tbsp pomegranate seeds
200g/7oz fresh raspberries, puréed
2–3 drops rosewater essence

Menjar blanc is a Catalan almond cream with medieval origins. It was documented in the oldest Catalan cookbook dating from 1324 and is now found in various guises all over the Mediterranean and beyond. In Menorca, it is traditionally thickened with rice flour and flavoured with vanilla.

In a heavy saucepan, bring the milk, almonds and vanilla pod to a boil, then reduce the heat and simmer for 3–4 minutes. Remove from the heat and let cool.

Pass the cooled almond milk through a fine sieve (strainer) into a measuring jug. Pour 100ml/3½fl oz/scant ½ cup of the milk into a separate bowl and mix in the cornflour (cornstarch).

Return the remaining milk to the saucepan, add the sugar, cinnamon stick and lemon zest and bring to a boil. Whisk in the cornflour-milk mixture and stir constantly until the milk starts to thicken. Remove the cinnamon stick and pour

the almond milk into glasses, ramekins or pudding moulds. Chill in the refrigerator for 4–6 hours or overnight.

Meanwhile, make the pomegranate syrup. In a small saucepan over a medium heat, stir together the water, pomegranate molasses and sugar for 5 minutes, or until the sugar dissolves. Bring to the boil, then simmer for 1–2 minutes until the syrup starts to thicken. Stir in the pomegranate seeds, raspberry purée and rosewater essence. Chill in the refrigerator until required.

To serve, carefully run the tip of a sharp knife around the edges of the moulds and turn out the almond creams onto small dessert plates. Spoon around the pomegranate syrup and garnish with fresh mint leaves.

SWEET POTATO *and* ALMOND *BUÑUELOS with* APRICOT *and* BEE POLLEN SAUCE

Cooking time: 50 minutes for baking sweet potatoes, plus 16–24 minutes for frying *buñuelos*
Preparation time: 20 minutes
Serves 6 (makes about 36–48 buñuelos)

--- **FOR THE *BUÑUELOS*:**
500g/1lb 2oz sweet potatoes, baked in their skins and cooled
1 egg
2 egg yolks
150g/5½oz/1½ cups ground almonds
50g/1¾oz/scant ½ cup icing (confectioners') sugar
1 pinch ground cinnamon
vegetable oil, for deep-frying
caster (superfine) sugar, for sprinkling

--- **FOR THE APRICOT AND BEE POLLEN SAUCE:**
200ml/7fl oz/scant 1 cup water
100g/3½oz/½ cup caster (superfine) sugar
500g/1lb 2oz fresh apricots, pitted
1 tbsp bee pollen
1 vanilla pod, split

Buñuelos, or bunyols as they are known in Mallorca, are simple, deep-fried doughnuts traditionally associated with fiestas and religious festivals. They are extremely popular at Easter and are flavoured with almonds or pine nuts, honey, cinnamon, and orange blossom water, reflecting their Arabian roots. The sweet potatoes are best cooked the day before, to allow them to dry out a little overnight.

Bee pollen is found in market stalls all over the island. It is considered one of nature's most nourishing foods and adds a slightly floral, nutty and bittersweet flavour to the finished sauce. It is readily available in most health food stores or online.

To make the apricot and bee pollen sauce, combine all the ingredients in a medium saucepan over a low heat and simmer for 20 minutes. Pass through a fine sieve (strainer) into a bowl and refrigerate until required.

To make the *buñuelos*, peel the baked and cooled sweet potatoes, place the flesh in a large bowl and work to a smooth purée with a wooden spoon. Mix in the egg and egg yolks, then add the ground almonds, sugar and cinnamon, beating well until the mixture forms a smooth dough. Set aside to rest for 30 minutes.

Heat enough oil for deep-frying in a deep, heavy saucepan to 190°C/375°F, or until a cube of bread browns in 30 seconds. Using two spoons dipped in hot water, form small balls of dough and lower them carefully into the hot oil. Working in batches of no more than 5 or 6 at a time, cook for 2–3 minutes, until golden brown all over, gently turning with a slotted spoon if necessary so that they cook evenly. Remove with a slotted spoon to drain on paper towels. Repeat until all the dough is used up, but be careful not to heat the oil too much, otherwise the *buñuelos* will be raw inside when cooked on the outside.

Sprinkle the *buñuelos* with a little caster (superfine) sugar and serve warm, about 6–8 per person, with the chilled apricot and bee pollen sauce.

MALLORCAN ALMOND CAKE *with* ORANGE BLOSSOM *and* KUMQUATS

Cooking time: 45-50 minutes
Preparation time: 20 minutes
Serves 8–10

butter or olive oil, for greasing
8 egg yolks
350g/12oz/1¾ cups caster
    (superfine) sugar
grated zest of 1 lemon
1 pinch ground cinnamon
500g/1lb 2oz/5 cups ground
    almonds
6 egg whites
25g/1oz/scant ¼ cup icing
    (confectioners') sugar, for
    dusting
vanilla ice cream, to serve
    (optional)

--- **FOR THE SYRUP**
15–20 fresh kumquats, halved
300ml/10½fl oz/1¼ cups orange
    juice
100ml/3½fl oz/scant ½ cup water
200g/7fl oz/1 cup caster
    (superfine) sugar
2–3 drops orange blossom syrup

Preheat the oven to 180°C/350°F/gas mark 4 and grease a deep-sided 20cm/8in cake pan with butter or olive oil.

In a large bowl, whisk together the egg yolks and caster (superfine) sugar with an electric hand whisk (beater) until the mixture is light and fluffy. Add the lemon zest, cinnamon and almonds and gently fold in until just combined. Set aside.

In a separate bowl and using a clean whisk, whisk the egg whites to stiff peaks, then add to the egg yolk mixture and carefully fold in until just combined. Pour the mixture into the prepared cake pan, then bake in the oven for 45–50 minutes, until golden and well risen. Turn off the oven and leave the door ajar while the cake cools to room temperature.

While the cake is cooling, make the kumquat syrup. Combine all the ingredients in a medium saucepan over a medium heat and bring to the boil, then reduce the heat to low and simmer for 4–5 minutes, stirring occasionally, until the mixture starts to thicken. Remove from the heat and set aside until the cake is ready to serve.

Carefully remove the cooled cake from the pan and dust with icing (confectioners') sugar. Slice into portions and place each portion on a serving plate. Spoon over the syrup and serve. For an extra decadent touch, serve with a scoop of vanilla ice cream on the side.

FIG *and* ALMOND TART

Cooking time: 30–35 minutes
Preparation time: 30 minutes,
plus chilling
Serves 8

10 fresh figs, halved lengthways
20 whole almonds, freshly peeled
icing (confectioners') sugar, for
    dusting
whipped cream or vanilla ice
    cream, to serve

--- FOR THE SWEET PASTRY:
200g/7oz/1¾ sticks cold butter,
    diced
450g/1lb/scant 3½ cups plain (all-
    purpose) flour, plus extra for
    dusting
1 pinch salt
150g/5oz/1¼ cups icing
    (confectioners') sugar
3 egg yolks

--- FOR THE FRANGIPANE:
6 egg yolks
130g/4½oz/⅔ cup caster
    (superfine) sugar
150g/5oz/1½ cups ground almonds
50g/1¾oz/generous ⅓ cup plain
    (all-purpose) flour
1½ tbsp cornflour (cornstarch)
500ml/17fl oz/2 cups milk
1 vanilla pod, split

To make the pastry, place the butter, flour and salt in a food processor and pulse until the mixture resembles breadcrumbs. Add the sugar and egg yolks and pulse again, just enough to incorporate the eggs. Scrape out the pastry and wrap in cling film (plastic wrap), then chill in the refrigerator for at least 30 minutes.

Roll out the pastry on a lightly floured surface to about 3mm/1/8inch thick. Line a 20 cm/8 in round tart pan with the pastry and rest in the refrigerator for at least 20 minutes.

To make the frangipane, place the egg yolks and sugar in a bowl and whisk until light and fluffy. Add the ground almonds, flour and cornflour (cornstarch) and mix well.

In a heavy saucepan, bring the milk to the boil with the vanilla pod. As soon as the milk starts to bubble, pour half into the egg yolk mixture, stirring all the time. Pour this mixture back into the pan with the milk and return to a low heat. Cook for 2–3 minutes, stirring continuously, until thickened. Pass the thick custard through a fine sieve (strainer) into a clean bowl and leave to cool.

Meanwhile, preheat the oven to 180°C/350°F/gas mark 4.

When cool, spoon the frangipane over the pastry case and level the surface with a palette knife. Press the figs lightly into the filling. Scatter the peeled almonds on top and dust with icing sugar.

Bake for 25–30 minutes, until the frangipane is cooked and the top is lightly caramelised. Serve when still slightly warm, with whipped cream or a scoop of vanilla ice cream.

ROASTED PEARS *in* ALMOND CRUMBS *with* CINNAMON-BRANDY CARAMEL SAUCE

Cooking time: 25 minutes
Preparation time: 20 minutes
Serves 4

4 large pears (Comice, Conference
   or Packham)
60g/2oz/½ cup finely chopped
   almonds
25g/1oz/¼ cup finely chopped
   pistachio nuts
2 tbsp brown (light muscovado)
   sugar
butter, for greasing
vanilla ice cream, to serve

--- **FOR THE POACHING LIQUID:**
1.2l/40fl oz/5 cups water
500g/1lb 2oz/2½ cups caster
   (superfine) sugar
juice of 3 lemons
1 cinnamon stick

--- **FOR THE CINNAMON-BRANDY
CARAMEL SAUCE:**
400ml/14fl oz/1⅔ cups poaching
   liquid from the pears
1 cinnamon stick
100ml/3½fl oz/scant ½ cup brandy
200ml/7fl oz/scant 1 cup double
   (heavy) cream

Carefully peel the pears, removing the skin but leaving the stalk on. Using a melon-baller, scoop out and remove the core from each pear, forming a small cavity.

In a stainless-steel saucepan, bring all the ingredients for the poaching liquid to the boil, add the pears and gently poach for 6–8 minutes. Remove from the heat and set aside to cool.

To make the sauce, strain off 400ml/14fl oz/1⅔ cups of the pear poaching liquid. Transfer it to a separate saucepan, bring to the boil, then reduce until it starts to bubble and caramelise, about 5 minutes. Add the cinnamon stick and remove the pan from the heat. Carefully stir in the brandy and cream, mix well and return to the heat. Bring back to the boil, then remove from the heat and whisk until smooth. Pass the sauce through a fine sieve (strainer) and set aside until ready to serve.

Meanwhile, preheat the oven to 180°C/350°F/gas mark 4 and grease a baking sheet with butter.

In a shallow bowl, mix the chopped almonds and pistachios with the brown (light muscovado) sugar. Roll the pears in the mixture until evenly covered and place on the greased baking sheet. Roast the pears in the oven for 6–8 minutes.

Carefully place the pears on 4 serving plates and serve with the cinnamon-brandy caramel sauce and vanilla ice cream.

Chocolate

Few people fail to realize the charms of chocolate. It is probably one of our most popular ingredients. Indeed, many food scientists have reported chocolate to be the single most craved food worldwide.

I'm a confessed chocoholic, and dark, velvety chocolate is my particular vice. Dark (bittersweet) chocolate is made without milk and should contain a minimum of 35% cocoa solids, at least 18% of which should be cocoa butter. I prefer mine to be around 70–75% for rich cakes, sauces or desserts.

Once known as "the food of the gods" in Aztec culture, the story of chocolate really began with Columbus and the discovery of the Americas. No one could ever have imagined how important the bitter cocoa beans would become. In the sixteenth and seventeenth centuries, chocolate was the favoured drink in nearly all of Spain's private houses. Even today, *chocolaterias* serving nothing but hot chocolate, churros and pastries still exist in most of Spain's major cities.

In recent years, Spanish pastry chefs have been at the forefront of a movement challenging the boundaries of chocolate work and pushing imaginative chocolate desserts to new heights, inventing crazy marriages such as chocolate and bacon, or pairing it with beetroot (beets), avocado, chilli, lavender and even cauliflower. Chocolate also finds its way into various savoury dishes throughout Spain and it is often served with game such as partridge, quail, hare and venison.

WHITE CHOCOLATE SOUP *with* CARAMELISED FIGS

Cooking time: 10 minutes
Preparation time: 10 minutes,
plus chilling
Serves 4

250ml/9fl oz/1 cup double (heavy) cream
100ml/3½fl oz/scant ½ cup milk
200g/7oz good-quality white chocolate, chopped
100ml/3½fl oz/scant ½ cup plain yogurt
1 lime: zest of ½ and juice of whole
4 fresh figs
2 tbsp brown sugar

The texture of this delicious soup is deliciously smooth and velvety, and it couldn't be simpler to make.

In a medium saucepan, bring the cream and milk to the boil, then remove from the heat and add the white chocolate. When the chocolate has completely dissolved, add the yogurt, lime juice and zest and stir well to combine. Chill in the refrigerator for at least 2 hours.

When ready to serve, cut the fresh figs in half and sprinkle with a little brown sugar. Caramelise with a kitchen blowtorch or under a hot grill (broiler).

Divide the white chocolate soup between 4 soup bowls and top each with 2 caramelised fig halves. Serve immediately.

CHURROS *with* HOT CHOCOLATE *and* ORANGE BLOSSOM DIP

Cooking time: 25 minutes
Preparation time: 10 minutes
Serves 4 (makes about 20 churros)

--- **FOR THE CHURROS:**
250ml/9fl oz/1 cup water
125g/4½ oz/generous 1 stick
   unsalted butter
1 wide strip lemon zest
200g/7oz/1½ cups plain
   (all-purpose) flour
1 egg
vegetable oil, for deep-frying
4 tbsp granulated sugar,
   for dusting
¼ tsp ground cinnamon,
   for dusting (optional)

--- **FOR THE HOT CHOCOLATE
AND ORANGE BLOSSOM DIP:**
250g/9oz dark (bittersweet)
   chocolate, chopped
grated zest of ½ orange
300ml/10½fl oz/1¼ cups milk
1 tsp cornflour (cornstarch)
2–3 drops orange blossom essence

There is no doubting that churros have become a part of Spain's social fabric, much like croissants in France and bagels in New York. They are easily the country's most popular fairground snack, hangover cure, and New Year's Eve treat. It has been that way for centuries, and this fried snack has become so universally adored that today it unites people of every walk of life. If you want to see a true cross-section of Spanish society, spend a few hours in a churrería or chocolate house.

To make the hot chocolate dip, gently heat the chocolate, orange zest and half of the milk together in a saucepan over a low heat, stirring until the chocolate has melted. Dissolve the cornflour (cornstarch) in the remaining milk and whisk into the melted chocolate. Continue to cook over a low heat, whisking constantly, until the chocolate has thickened, about 1–2 minutes. Add the orange blossom essence and keep warm until ready to serve.

To make the churros, combine the water, butter and lemon zest in a saucepan and bring to the boil. Remove and discard the lemon zest. Reduce the heat to low and add the flour, stirring vigorously until the mixture comes cleanly away from the sides of the pan and forms a ball, about 1 minute. Remove the pan from the heat and beat in the whole egg. Continue beating until the batter is thick and smooth.

Spoon the batter into a piping bag fitted with a medium-sized (2.5cm/1in) fluted or star-shaped piping nozzle.

Heat enough oil for deep-frying in a deep, heavy saucepan to 190°C/375°F, or until a cube of bread browns in 30 seconds. Carefully pipe 10 cm/4 in strips of dough directly into the hot oil, snipping them off cleanly with a pair of kitchen scissors. Fry for about 2 minutes on each side, turning once, until golden brown. Fry 3 or 4 strips at a time and remove with tongs to drain on paper towels.

Sprinkle the hot churros with sugar and cinnamon, if using. Serve with the hot chocolate and orange blossom dipping sauce, poured into 4 individual serving cups.

CHOCOLATE *and* LAVENDER TART

Cooking time: 30 minutes
Preparation time: 20 minutes,
plus chilling
Serves 6–8

--- **FOR THE PASTRY:**

50g/1¾oz/3½ tbsp chilled unsalted
    butter, diced
120g/4½oz/scant 1 cup plain (all-
    purpose) flour, plus extra for
    dusting
1 pinch sea salt
60g/2oz/½ cup icing
    (confectioners') sugar
1 egg
1 tbsp cold water

--- **FOR THE FILLING:**

100g/3½oz/scant 1 stick unsalted
    butter
180g/6½oz dark (bittersweet)
    chocolate, chopped
1 tbsp dried lavender flowers
140g/5oz/scant ¾ cup caster
    (superfine) sugar
80g/2¾oz/scant ⅔ cup plain (all-
    purpose) flour
6 eggs

--- **TO SERVE:**

2 tbsp dark unsweetened cocoa
    powder, for dusting
vanilla ice cream
fresh berries

To make the pastry, combine the butter, flour and salt in a food processor and pulse until the mixture resembles breadcrumbs. Add the sugar, egg and cold water and pulse again to incorporate the egg. Scrape out the pastry and knead gently to form a firm dough. Wrap in cling film (plastic wrap) and chill for at least 30 minutes.

Roll the pastry out to 3mm/1/8in thick on a lightly floured surface. Line a 23cm/9in loose-bottomed tart pan with the pastry and chill for at least 20 minutes.

Meanwhile, preheat the oven to 200°C/400°F/gas mark 6.

Prick the base of the chilled pastry case with a fork, line with baking parchment and fill with baking beans (pie weights). Blind bake for 10 minutes, or until lightly golden brown, then remove the paper and baking beans and return to the oven to bake for a further 3–4 minutes.

To make the filling, gently heat the butter, chocolate and lavender flowers in a medium saucepan over a low heat, stirring until melted and smooth. Remove from the heat and stir in the sugar and flour. Beat in the eggs, one at a time. Pass the mixture through a fine sieve (strainer).

Place the pastry case (still in the tart pan) on a baking sheet and pour the filling mixture into the pastry case, filling it right to the top. Bake for 12–15 minutes, or until just set. Remove from the oven and let cool completely in the pan, before removing it. Dust with cocoa powder, cut into portions and serve with vanilla ice cream and fresh berries.

CHOCOLATE, CARDAMOM *and* COFFEE CREAMS *with* ORANGE *and* CINNAMON TUILES

Cooking time: 50 minutes
Preparation time: 20 minutes,
plus chilling/cooling
Serves 6–8

--- **FOR THE TUILES:**
50g/1¾oz/3½ tbsp unsalted butter
150g/5¼oz/scant 1¼ cups plain (all-
    purpose) flour
100g/3½oz/½ cup caster
    (superfine) sugar
1 pinch ground cinnamon
grated zest of 1 orange
100g/3½oz/⅓ cup golden syrup

--- **FOR THE CHOCOLATE,**
CARDAMOM AND COFFEE CREAMS:
50g/1¾oz/⅓ cup coffee beans
4 cardamom pods, lightly crushed
½ cinnamon stick
300ml/10½fl oz/1¼ cups double
    (heavy) cream
80g/3oz dark (bittersweet)
    chocolate
5 egg yolks
180g/6oz/scant 1 cup caster
    (superfine) sugar
lightly whipped cream, to serve

To make the tuiles, gently melt the butter in a pan. Combine the flour, sugar, cinnamon and orange zest in a bowl, then add the golden syrup. Whisk in the melted butter, cover and chill for 30 minutes.

Meanwhile, preheat the oven to 200°C/400°F/ gas mark 6 and line a baking sheet with baking parchment.

Place 3 teaspoons of the tuile mixture on the baking sheet, well spaced, and spread out to 8cm/3in circles. Bake in the oven for 6–8 minutes, or until golden brown. Remove from the oven and use a metal spatula to quickly and carefully drape each tuile over a rolling pin, then let rest until they are cool and crisp. Remove the tuiles to a cooling rack. Cook the remaining tuiles in the same way, until all the mixture has been used up. As soon as the tuiles are cool, store in an airtight container to keep them crisp until ready to serve.

To make the creams, heat a frying pan (skillet) over a low heat and toast the coffee beans, cardamom pods and cinnamon stick until fragrant. Transfer to a spice grinder or food processor and grind to a coarse powder. In a saucepan, combine the cream with the coffee-spice mixture and bring slowly to the boil, then reduce the heat and simmer for 2–3 minutes. Remove from the heat and leave to cool and infuse for 10–15 minutes.

Pass the cooled cream through a fine sieve (strainer) into a clean saucepan and return to a low heat. Add the chocolate and stir until it has melted. Whisk the egg yolks and sugar in a bowl until pale and fluffy, then add to the warm chocolate mixture. Heat gently, stirring continuously, until the mixture thickens into a custard, about 1–2 minutes. Pour the custard into coffee cups or glasses and chill well for about 4 hours.

Serve topped with a little lightly whipped cream and garnished with orange and cinnamon tuiles.

CHOCOLATE *and* OLIVE OIL TRUFFLE *with* FLOR DE SAL *and a* RASPBERRY *and* RED PEPPER JELLY

Cooking time: 10 minutes
Preparation time: 20 minutes, plus chilling
Serves 12

--- **FOR THE SUGAR SYRUP:**
75ml/2½fl oz/⅓ cup water
75g/2½oz/⅓ cup caster (superfine) sugar

--- **FOR THE RASPBERRY AND RED PEPPER JELLY:**
5 gelatine leaves
75ml/2½fl oz/⅓ cup sugar syrup (see above)
275g/10oz roasted red peppers, peeled and deseeded
300g/10½oz raspberries, puréed
2 tsp raspberry vinegar

--- **FOR THE TRUFFLE:**
300ml/10½fl oz/1¼ cups single (light) cream
400ml/14fl oz/1 ⅔ cups milk
4 tsp orange liqueur (such as Grand Marnier)
350g/12oz dark (bittersweet) chocolate, broken into small pieces
150g/5½oz milk chocolate, broken into small pieces
200ml/7fl oz/scant 1 cup extra virgin olive oil
flor de sal (or sea salt), to garnish
fresh raspberries, to garnish

This has become one of our signature desserts at the restaurant. It may look a little complicated, but it's actually a really simple dessert that can be prepared well in advance and plated quickly. The sweet, salty and sour combinations in this dessert are pleasantly surprising; the grains of flor de sal sea salt are optional, but they really do jerk your tastebuds to life when you bite into one.

To make the sugar syrup, bring the water and sugar slowly to a boil in a saucepan set over a medium heat. Stir constantly until the sugar dissolves completely and the mixture is clear, about 1–2 minutes. Remove from the heat and chill in the refrigerator until required or use immediately.

To make the jelly, soften the gelatine leaves in a little cold water. In a saucepan, bring the sugar syrup to the boil. Squeeze the excess water out of the gelatine leaves and add to the sugar syrup, then remove from the heat and whisk until the gelatine has completely dissolved. Add the red peppers, raspberry purée and vinegar. Purée in a food processor or with a hand-held (immersion) blender, then pass through a fine sieve (strainer) into a plastic container. Chill in the refrigerator for at least 6 hours or overnight until set.

To make the truffle, bring the cream, milk and orange liqueur to the boil in a large saucepan, then remove from the heat. Add both chocolates to the warm cream and stir until dissolved. Whisk in the olive oil until well combined, then pour the mixture into a plastic container. Chill in the refrigerator for at least 6 hours or overnight until set.

To serve, cut the jelly into small cubes. Place a spoonful of truffle mixture on each dessert plate, sprinkle with a little *flor de sal* and decorate with 3–4 cubes of jelly and some fresh raspberries.

Chorizo

I love traditional Spanish cooking, with its intoxicating aromas and delicious flavours – it is uncomplicated food based on simple ingredients. One of those ingredients is chorizo, the quintessential Spanish sausage.

Thought to have originated in Extremadura, the original chorizo was a rather pale-looking specimen, as it was not until the conquistadors introduced red pepper from the New World that it started to resemble the dark red, smoky pork sausage that we enjoy today. Other ingredients, along with pork and pork fat, include salt, and occasionally white wine, sugar or sherry. The latter aid in the fermentation process, which gives chorizo its typical slightly tangy and acidic taste. A pork and lard mixture is marinated for one to two days in the seasonings, and is then stuffed into casings made either from pigs' intestines or synthetic ones of collagen or plant cellulose. The sausages are then hung to dry and cure for a minimum of three months. In some wetter parts of Spain, they are lightly smoked before hanging. The final product is usually given one of the following shapes: *vela* (long, thin and straight), *ristra* (small and tied together) or *sarta* (U-shaped). The best chorizos are labelled "*Ibérico*"; these are made from free-range Iberian black-legged pigs that graze on acorns.

Chorizo works well with squid, octopus and scallops, combines perfectly with potatoes and is found in an array of Spanish egg and rice dishes. It also flavours many of Spain's classic *potajes* (one-pot dishes), from the delicious *fabada Asturiana* to the rustic, heart-warming *cocido Madrileño*.

FENNEL, CHORIZO *and* TARRAGON SOUP

Cooking time: 35 minutes
Preparation time: 20 minutes
Serves 6

2 tbsp olive oil
1 onion, finely chopped
2 garlic cloves, crushed
3 medium fennel bulbs, cored and
    chopped
75g/2½oz chorizo, skinned and
    chopped, plus some extra slices
    for garnish
1l/35fl oz/4¼ cups chicken stock
    (bouillon)
200ml/7fl oz/scant 1 cup double
    (heavy) cream
juice of 1 lime
2 tbsp chopped fresh tarragon,
    plus a few leaves for garnish
sea salt and white pepper

Heat the olive oil in a large saucepan over a low heat, add the onion, garlic and fennel and cook for 2–3 minutes, until softened but not coloured. Add the chorizo and chicken stock (bouillon) and bring to the boil, then reduce the heat to low, cover and simmer for 30 minutes.

Add the cream, lime juice and tarragon, then blend to a smooth purée in a food processor or with a hand-held (immersion) blender. Season to taste with salt and white pepper, then pass through a fine sieve (strainer).

Ladle into soup bowls and garnish with a couple of chorizo slices and fresh tarragon leaves. Serve immediately.

SIMPLE SCRAMBLED EGGS *with* WILD MUSHROOMS *and* CHORIZO

Cooking time: 7 minutes
Preparation time: 5 minutes
Serves 4

2 tbsp olive oil
100g/3½oz chorizo, diced
1 garlic clove, crushed
175g/6oz mixed wild mushrooms, cleaned and diced
8 eggs, beaten
2 tbsp double (heavy) cream
1 tbsp chopped flat-leaf parsley
sea salt and freshly ground black pepper

Heat the olive oil in a non-stick frying pan (skillet) over a medium heat and sauté the chorizo, garlic and mushrooms until they begin to brown and soften. Add the beaten eggs to the pan and cook, stirring with a wooden spoon, until just set, about 1 minute. Remove from the heat and stir in the cream and chopped parsley. Season to taste and serve immediately.

POOR MAN'S
POTATOES
with CHORIZO

Cooking time: 10 minutes
Preparation time: 20 minutes
Serves 4

200ml/7fl oz/scant 1 cup olive oil
500g/1lb 2oz boiled floury
    potatoes, cut into 4cm/1½in
    chunks
200g/7oz cooking chorizo, diced
3 garlic cloves, crushed
2 sprigs fresh thyme
4 eggs
2 tbsp chopped flat-leaf parsley
1 tsp sweet paprika (preferably
    Mallorcan *Tap de Cortí*), plus
    extra for dusting
sea salt and freshly ground black
    pepper

Heat about 175ml/6fl oz/¾ cup of the olive oil in a non-stick frying pan (skillet) over a medium heat and fry the potatoes until they start to colour. Add the diced chorizo, garlic and fresh thyme and continue to fry, until the potatoes and chorizo are nicely coloured and starting to crisp up, about 4–5 minutes.

Meanwhile, fry the eggs in a separate pan in the remaining olive oil.

Add the chopped parsley and paprika to the potatoes and season to taste. Divide the potatoes between 4 plates and top each with a fried egg. Dust with more paprika and serve immediately.

GRILLED RAZOR CLAMS *with* CHORIZO, BROAD BEANS *and* TOMATOES

Cooking time: 10 minutes
Preparation time: 15 minutes
Serves 4

1kg/2lb 3oz live razor clams
250g/9oz broad (fava) beans, shelled
6 tbsp olive oil
115g/4oz cooking chorizo, skinned and diced
200g/7oz tomatoes, diced
1 tbsp chopped flat-leaf parsley
3 garlic cloves, roughly chopped
few sprigs fresh thyme, leaves stripped
120ml/4fl oz/½ cup dry white wine
sea salt and freshly ground black pepper
crusty bread, to serve
lemon wedges, to serve

Razor clams are absolutely delicious and combine brilliantly with chorizo. It is necessary to properly clean and prepare razor clams before cooking. This takes a little time, as each razor clam needs to be checked individually, but it is well worth the effort.

Wash the razor clams quickly under running water (do not soak in water for too long as this will spoil them). Check that all the clams are closed and that the shells are not damaged or cracked in any way. If open, the shells should close when gently tapped; if they don't, they should be discarded.

Cook the broad (fava) beans in boiling salted water for 2 minutes, then drain in a colander and set aside.

Heat 4 tablespoons of the olive oil in a frying pan (skillet) over a low heat, add the chorizo and cook for 1–2 minutes. Add the broad beans, diced tomatoes and chopped parsley, and season lightly with salt and pepper.

Heat a griddle (grill) pan until very hot. Place the razor clams on the griddle, drizzle with a little olive oil and cook for about 2–3 minutes, until the shells begin to open. Sprinkle over the garlic and thyme leaves and cook for a further 30 seconds, then remove from the heat and pour over the white wine. Spoon the chorizo mixture over the clams and drizzle with a little more olive oil. Serve piping hot with crusty bread and lemon wedges.

SPICY CHICKEN *and* HARISSA RAGOUT *with* SMOKED CHORIZO

Cooking time: 40 minutes
Preparation time: 15 minutes
Serves 4

3 tbsp olive oil
1 red onion, chopped
2 garlic cloves, crushed
110g/4oz smoked chorizo, chopped
600g/1lb 5oz skinless, boneless
    chicken thighs
300ml/10½fl oz/1¼ cups chicken
    stock (bouillon)
350g/12oz canned chopped
    tomatoes
2 tsp harissa paste
juice of 1 lemon
2 tbsp chopped fresh coriander
    (cilantro)
150g/5½oz/scant ¾ cup plain
    yogurt
sea salt and freshly ground black
    pepper
cooked rice or couscous, to serve

Heat the olive oil in a large, heavy saucepan over a low-medium heat, add the onion and garlic and cook for 1 minute. Add the smoked chorizo, chicken thighs, chicken stock (bouillon), chopped tomatoes and harissa paste and cook, covered, for 35–40 minutes, or until the sauce has thickened.

Remove from the heat and stir in the lemon juice, chopped coriander (cilantro) and yogurt. Season to taste and serve with cooked rice or couscous.

LOTE:
17030

SOBRASADA

Unlike many of the other incredible ingredients that are native to Mallorca (red prawns, truffles, langoustines and aged Iberian ham, to name just a few), my relationship with *sobrasada*, a soft and spicy cured sausage traditional on the Balearic Islands, was far from love at first sight – or, indeed, taste.

In fact, my first impression was of a relic of a past time that existed only out of necessity – *sobrasada* was often the only meat available to most people for much of the year, and its unusual spreadable texture was a result of Mallorca's unique combination of high humidity and cool temperature during the winter months (when the pigs were traditionally put to slaughter). I viewed it as an outdated lump of pork fat flavoured with paprika that belonged more in a museum than anywhere near my food, but the truth is that I was very, very wrong.

As time passed and I came to know more about the island and the story of its food, I came across the sausage more and more and grew to appreciate its wonderful smokiness and its capacity to add flavour to so many recipes, such as the delicious croquettes on page 50. You can also stir it into risotto, add it to mashed potatoes, or combine it with breadcrumbs and herbs to make a delicious crust for wonderfully juicy and fragrant roast pork (see page 72).

The making of *sobrasada* goes back to ancient times, and it was a staple in most sixteenth-century Mallorcan households, but recently it has been undergoing somewhat of a renaissance, with forward-thinking butchers such as my friend Xesc Reina reinventing it with new flavour profiles and making this old Mallorcan classic feel like something very modern indeed.

You can buy *sobrasada* easily online and in Mediterranean delis. Some of the larger supermarkets now stock it, sometimes marketed as "spreadable chorizo", or Italian *'nduja* also makes a good alternative.

CRISPY SOBRASADA CROQUETTES *with* HONEY *and* MANCHEGO

Cooking time: 45 minutes
Preparation time: 30 minutes,
plus chilling
Serves 4 (makes 12–15 croquettes)

vegetable oil, for frying
Aioli (see page 55), to serve

--- FOR THE FILLING:
500ml/17fl oz/2 cups milk
1 small onion, finely chopped
1 bay leaf
6 black peppercorns
60g/2oz/½ stick unsalted butter
2 tbsp olive oil
60g/2oz/scant ½ cup plain (all-purpose) flour
130g/4½oz sobrasada, at room temperature
1 tbsp clear honey
2 tbsp finely chopped flat-leaf parsley
sea salt and freshly ground black pepper

--- FOR THE COATING:
2 eggs
150g/5½oz/3 cups breadcrumbs (panko, if possible)
25g/1oz cured Manchego cheese, finely grated
60g/2oz/scant ½ cup plain (all-purpose) flour
sea salt and freshly ground black pepper

*The perfect **tapa** to enjoy with a cold beer, sun on your face and good company.*

Bring the milk to the boil in a saucepan, along with the onion, bay leaf and the peppercorns. Set aside to infuse for 10 minutes, then strain.

Melt the butter and olive oil together in a medium saucepan over a low heat. Stir in the flour and cook for 3–4 minutes, until smooth. Add a little of the strained milk, stirring until smooth, then add a little more. Continue until the milk is used up and the sauce has thickened. Add the *sobrasada* and honey and cook for 10–15 minutes, whisking regularly, until you have a smooth, thick béchamel-type sauce.

Stir in the chopped parsley, season with salt and black pepper, then transfer to a shallow container and cover with cling film (plastic wrap) to prevent a skin forming. Allow to cool to room temperature, then chill in the refrigerator for a minimum of 4 hours or overnight, until set.

To make the coating, beat the eggs in a bowl. Add the breadcrumbs and grated cheese to a second bowl, stirring to combine. Add the flour to a third bowl, seasoning well with salt and pepper. Dusting your hands with some of the flour, scoop out a heaped tablespoon of the firm filling mixture and roll it into a ball, then roll in the seasoned flour until covered. Dip it into the egg, followed by the breadcrumbs, and set aside on a baking sheet. Repeat until all the mixture is used up. Chill for at least 20 minutes.

Heat enough oil for shallow-frying in a large frying pan (skillet) over a medium heat. In batches of 5 or 6, shallow-fry the croquettes, turning regularly, until crisp and golden brown, about 2–3 minutes. Alternatively, heat enough oil for deep-frying in a deep, heavy saucepan to 180°C/350°F, or until a cube of bread browns in 30 seconds, and deep-fry the croquettes for 3–4 minutes. Drain well on paper towels.

Serve piping hot, with some aioli for dipping.

Garlic

AJO

Nothing beats the mouthwatering aroma of garlic and onions sweating in olive oil. It's the first easy task of so many Mediterranean recipes and it fills any kitchen with the most tantalising, intoxicating fragrance.

Spanish restaurants are awash with garlic, from olives marinated with it, to classic aioli (see page 55) and gazpacho (see page 134), to clams and *gambas al ajillo* (prawns/shrimp with garlic – see page 175). In spring, wild garlic grows all over the island and tender, young green garlic shoots known as *ajos tiernos* are grilled (broiled) and sprinkled with olive oil and sea salt or are finely chopped and stirred into scrambled eggs. And for those who aren't keen on the pungency of raw garlic, there are plenty of recipes where long, slow cooking mellows it.

Garlic was once so highly prized that it was used as currency and the Egyptians worshipped it so much that they placed clay models of garlic bulbs in the tomb of Tutankhamun. Recent studies have shown that garlic lowers cholesterol, reduces the risk of heart disease, fights infection and boosts immunity. I could also mention the alleged aphrodisiacal powers of garlic, which have been extolled through the ages, but – for me – it's all about that amazing, heavenly aroma.

"COLOURED GARLIC" DIP

Cooking time: 15–20 minutes
Preparation time: 20 minutes
Serves 4

1kg/2lb 3oz potatoes, peeled and
    diced
1 onion, finely chopped
1 red pepper, deseeded and diced
700ml/24fl oz/3 cups vegetable
    stock (bouillon)
4 garlic cloves, crushed
1 tbsp tomato purée (paste)
1 pinch paprika
1 pinch ground cumin
50ml/2fl oz/¼ cup olive oil
1 tbsp sherry vinegar
sea salt and freshly ground black
    pepper

*This sauce or dip from Almería
is traditionally served with
poached fish, but is also
delicious with grilled meats or
vegetables. It can be stored in an
airtight container or jar for 3–4
days in the refrigerator.*

Place the potatoes, onions and
red pepper in a large saucepan
and cover with vegetable stock
(bouillon). Bring to the boil and
simmer for 15–20 minutes.

Meanwhile, put the garlic, tomato
purée (paste), paprika and cumin
into a pestle and mortar and
pound to a smooth paste.

Drain the potatoes, onions
and peppers, transfer to a food
processor and blend to a paste.
With the motor running, slowly
pour the olive oil down the feed-
tube of the food processor to
emulsify and thicken the sauce,
then add the sherry vinegar.

Scoop the mixture out into a
bowl and stir through the garlic
paste. Season to taste and serve
while still warm, with crusty
bread for dipping.

AIOLI

Cooking time: N/A
Preparation time: 10 minutes
Serves 4

4 garlic cloves, chopped
2 egg yolks
250ml/9fl oz/1 cup olive oil
juice of ½ lemon
sea salt and freshly ground black
    pepper

Alioli means "garlic and oil" in Spanish, and it's probably the most popular sauce throughout the whole Mediterranean region. It's often served with toasted bread and marinated olives at the beginning of a meal and is indispensable with fried fish, squid and patatas bravas. I also love to mix a spoonful of aioli into traditional rice dishes to add flavour and a smooth, creamy texture.

In a pestle and mortar, crush the garlic cloves and a good pinch of salt to a fine paste. Transfer to a large bowl and add the egg yolks, whisking until incorporated. Slowly add the olive oil, whisking continuously until the sauce thickens. Finally, whisk in the lemon juice, along with a few drops of water if it seems too thick. Season with salt and pepper to taste.

GRILLED ASPARAGUS *with* ORANGE DRESSING *and* ROMESCO SAUCE

Cooking time: 38–40 minutes
Preparation time: 30 minutes
Serves 4

24 asparagus stalks, peeled
coarse sea salt
olive oil, for brushing
small handful toasted almonds, to garnish

--- **FOR THE ROMESCO SAUCE:**
1 large red pepper
100g/3½oz/¾ cup peeled almonds, lightly toasted
3 garlic cloves, crushed
1 slice stale white bread
350ml/12fl oz/scant 1½ cups olive oil
1 tbsp tomato purée (paste)
2 tsp paprika
50ml/2fl oz/¼ cup brandy
2 tbsp sherry vinegar
sea salt and freshly ground black pepper

--- **FOR THE ORANGE DRESSING:**
juice of 2 oranges
100ml/3½fl oz/scant ½ cup olive oil
1 tsp sherry vinegar
1 tsp chopped chives
sea salt and freshly ground black pepper

Romesco is a sauce originating in Tarragona, Catalonia. You can substitute the almonds for hazelnuts, pine nuts or walnuts.

For grilling (broiling), you need fairly thick asparagus, not the thin type. Check the tips to make sure the asparagus hasn't begun to flower.

For the sauce, roast the red pepper in a hot oven or place under a hot grill (broiler) until the skin starts to blacken and blister, about 15 minutes. Place in a bowl, cover with cling film (plastic wrap) and set aside to cool for about 10 minutes – the steam will help to loosen the skin on the pepper. When cool enough to handle, cut the pepper in half lengthways, remove the seeds, and peel off and discard the skin. Place the pepper flesh in a food processor, along with the toasted almonds, garlic, stale bread and half of the olive oil and blend to a purée. Add the tomato purée (paste), paprika, brandy and sherry vinegar and whisk in the remaining olive oil to emulsify and thicken the sauce. Season to taste and chill in the refrigerator until required.

Blanch the asparagus in boiling salted water until the stalks are crisp and just al dente, 6–8 minutes. Drain and set aside.

For the orange dressing, bring the orange juice to the boil in a small saucepan and cook until reduced by half, about 15 minutes. Remove from the heat and whisk in the olive oil and sherry vinegar. Add the chopped chives and season to taste.

Brush the asparagus spears with olive oil and season with salt. Grill over hot coals or on a hot griddle (grill) pan, turning once, for just long enough to colour lightly and warm through, about 1 minute on each side. Serve the hot asparagus with the orange dressing, Romesco sauce and a scattering of toasted almonds.

BASQUE-STYLE SALT COD *in* PIL-PIL SAUCE

Cooking time: 8–10 minutes
Preparation time: 10 minutes,
plus 24 hours pre-soaking if needed
Serves 4

450ml/15fl oz/scant 2 cups olive oil
4 garlic cloves, sliced
½ red chilli, chopped
4 x 125g/4½oz salt cod fillets,
    pre-soaked and rinsed
sea salt and freshly ground black
    pepper

This is a classic salt cod recipe from the Basque country in northern Spain. The toasting of the garlic cloves in the hot olive oil is what gives the dish its unique flavour and aroma. The Basque people will proudly tell you that they accidently invented **bacalao** *(salted cod) when a group of Basque fishermen sailed from the Bay of Biscay in search of whales and came across a "field" of cod off the coast of Norway. Legend has it that they landed so much fish that their boats were overflowing. They were so far away from home that the only option was to fillet the cod and conserve it in salt, using the same technique for the conservation of whale meat.*

Before it can be cooked, salt cod needs pre-soaking in cold water for 24 hours, changing the water 2 or 3 times, although you can also buy it "ready-to-cook". Leave the skin on for this recipe as it helps to emulsify the sauce.

Heat the olive oil in a heavy frying pan (skillet) or round earthenware dish over a medium-low heat and gently fry the sliced garlic and red chilli until golden brown. Use a slotted spoon to remove the garlic and chilli and set aside.

Place the salt cod fillets skin-side up in the pan or dish and cook gently for 4–6 minutes. Turn the fillets over and remove from the heat. Pour the warm oil into a bowl or jug. Moving the pan or dish in a circular motion, slowly add the olive oil back in, to gradually emulsify the sauce until thick and translucent. Season to taste, then sprinkle over the reserved garlic and chilli. Serve immediately.

FRESH CLAMS *in* WHITE WINE *with* GARLIC *and* PARSLEY

Cooking time: 7 minutes
Preparation time: 10 minutes
Serves 4

2 tbsp olive oil
100g/3½oz onion, chopped
3 garlic cloves, crushed
50ml/2fl oz/¼ cup white wine
50ml/2fl oz/¼ cup fish stock
   (bouillon)
1kg/2lb 3oz fresh clams, well
   cleaned
2 tbsp chopped flat-leaf parsley
sea salt and freshly ground black
   pepper

Heat the olive oil in a heavy saucepan over a medium-low heat, add the onion and garlic and gently cook, until the onion has softened but not coloured. Add the white wine and fish stock (bouillon), increase the heat and bring to the boil. Add the clams, cover with a lid and cook for 1 minute, or until the clams have opened. Discard any clams that have not opened. Sprinkle with parsley and season to taste.

Divide the clams and broth between 4 warm soup bowls and serve immediately.

QUAILS STEWED *in* ONIONS, GARLIC *and* WHITE WINE

Cooking time: 40–45 minutes
Preparation time: 10 minutes
Serves 4

200ml/7 fl oz/scant 1 cup olive oil
8 quails
2 large onions (preferably
    Spanish), finely sliced
3 garlic cloves, crushed
sprig of fresh thyme
1 pinch paprika
2 bay leaves
200ml/7 fl oz/scant 1 cup dry
    white wine
1 tbsp sherry vinegar
2 tbsp finely chopped chives
sea salt and freshly ground black
    pepper

Heat half of the olive oil in a large, heavy saucepan over a medium-low heat and gently brown the quails on all sides. Remove the quails and set aside.

Add the remaining olive oil to the pan and add the onions. Gently cook for 3–4 minutes, stirring with a wooden spoon, until softened but not coloured. Add the garlic, thyme, paprika and bay leaves, then return the quails to the pan and stir well to coat the meat in the oil. Add the wine and sherry vinegar and cover with a lid. Cook over a gentle heat for 25–30 minutes, stirring occasionally.

Season with salt and pepper, sprinkle with chopped chives and serve immediately.

Iberian Pork
CERDO IBÉRICO

Pork is, perhaps, the supreme winter meat and has some wonderful cuts for grilling, braising, stuffing and roasting. Despite its prohibition by two major religions, pork is the world's most-consumed meat. Unfortunately, that means that it has to be mass-produced, and a lot of the meat on sale is intensively farmed, using hybrid breeds of animal that have been bred to grow rapidly and carry more meat, leaving little time for the meat to develop taste and texture. Meat from animals that have been allowed to mature slowly in happy surroundings, fed on natural or organic feed, will have a rich flavour that, if you can find it, makes it worth paying extra for.

Every year, I try to help our Spanish friends with their traditional *matanzas*, which literally translates as "the slaughter". I always arrive well after the pigs have met their maker but, even then, it is definitely not recommended for the squeamish. Like everything else in Spain, *La Matanza* is as good a reason as any for a fiesta. It takes place in a festive atmosphere with everyone from the village joining in to help out, preparing meat products to be stored for the coming year. The first thing you learn is that absolutely nothing goes to waste. Perishable meat is eaten immediately and washed down with copious amounts of alcohol. Every part of the animal is put to good use in the making of sausage-like *embutidos* (charcuterie); among these are *chorizo*, *salchichón*, *morcilla*, *butifarra* and, of course, *sobrasada*.

A CUT ABOVE

Spain is blessed with some top-quality ingredients, but if I had to choose one as the undisputed champion of Spanish gastronomy, it would have to be *jamón Ibérico de bellota*.

All hams are not created equal – it really is important to understand the subtle differences when you enter into the world of Spanish hams. The most basic, and therefore the cheapest, is simply called *jamón serrano*. *Serrano* means "sierra" or 'mountain' and there are many types available. It is generally made from white pigs, usually Landrace or Duroc breeds. The next step up is *jamón Ibérico*, made from farm-raised, usually cross-bred Ibérico pigs that are raised indoors and fed hay.

Jamón Ibérico de bellota is the premier level and has acquired a cult-like following throughout the world. The *cerdo Ibérico de bellota* are dark-coloured animals with longer legs and leaner haunches than the domestic pig. They roam free, feeding on acorns in the oak forests of Andalucía and Extremadura. These acorns impart an intense, aromatic flavour and give the finished ham its unmistakable rich taste and texture.

The art of producing top-quality hams is a complex process. The pigs' legs are first salted and then hung to mature for a period of between eighteen months to three years. The transformation from Iberian pig to world-renowned *jamón Ibérico de bellota* takes about five years: two years fattening the pigs and three years curing the meat. The best hams should have a shiny, dark red-brown colour, speckled with tiny white flecks from eating fatty acorns. They should be sliced into wafer-thin rashers from the leg and eaten immediately. A special support, a *jamonero*, is used for this, along with a very sharp knife with a long narrow blade. The ham should be served at room temperature and needs nothing more than crusty bread to accompany it.

Cured hams are used in Spanish cookery to flavour many soups and stews, as well as vegetable and egg dishes. If you're thinking of buying a whole ham, look for the metal stamp and the producer's guarantee. Price is a good indicator of quality and the top hams can fetch as much as 200 euros a kilo. It may sound like a lot, but we are talking about one of the great gastronomic delights of the world, and that kind of quality doesn't come cheap.

PORK LOIN BRAISED *in* MILK

Cooking time: 1 hour 10 minutes
Preparation time: 10 minutes
Serves 6

2 tbsp olive oil
1.2kg/2lb 12oz boneless pork loin,
    trimmed
100g/3½oz bacon, diced
5 garlic cloves, crushed
1 tbsp fresh thyme leaves, chopped
1l/35fl oz/4¼ cups milk
2 bay leaves
½ cinnamon stick
1 tbsp chopped flat-leaf parsley
sea salt and freshly ground black
    pepper

This is simple Spanish comfort food. Slowly braising the pork in milk tenderises the meat and adds a delicious, robust flavour to the finished sauce. In Italy, it is traditionally made with pork shoulder and known as maiale al latte. It's excellent served with creamy polenta or vegetables and new potatoes.

Heat the olive oil in a casserole dish (Dutch oven) over a low-medium heat. Sear the pork loin on both sides, then add the bacon, garlic and thyme. Pour over the milk, add the bay leaves and cinnamon stick, and season with salt and pepper. Cover with a lid, reduce the heat and simmer gently for about 1 hour, until the meat is very tender. Keep an eye on the milk during the cooking process, to prevent it from burning on the bottom of the pan.

Remove the pork loin, slice into portions and place on a serving platter or dish. Pass the milk through a fine sieve (strainer), return it to the casserole and bring back to the boil. Add the chopped parsley, adjust the seasoning and pour the milk over the sliced pork. Serve immediately.

MALLORCAN-STYLE STUFFED AUBERGINES

Cooking time: 30–40 minutes
Preparation time: 15 minutes
Serves 4

4 medium aubergines (eggplant),
    about 250g/9oz each
150ml/5fl oz/⅔ cup olive oil,
    plus extra for drizzling
250g/9oz minced (ground) pork
1 onion, finely chopped
3 garlic cloves, crushed
1 sprig fresh thyme
350g/12oz tomatoes, peeled,
    deseeded and chopped
1 tbsp tomato purée (paste)
1 tsp sweet paprika (preferably
    Mallorcan Tap de Cortí), plus
    extra for sprinkling
¼ tsp ground cinnamon
200ml/7fl oz/scant 1 cup white
    wine
1 tbsp plain (all-purpose) flour
200g/7oz Manchego cheese,
    grated
50g/1¾oz/1 cup fine breadcrumbs
sea salt and freshly ground black
    pepper

Stuffed aubergines (eggplant) are often served as a simple, family treat in Mallorca. The aubergine is such a wonderful vessel for capturing flavour, and when grilled (broiled) until crisp, stuffed and baked with melting Manchego cheese, what's not to love?

Preheat the grill (broiler) until hot and heat the oven to 200°C/400°F/gas mark 6.

Cut the aubergines (eggplant) in half lengthways and scoop out the flesh, leaving the shells about 1cm/½in thick. Chop the aubergine flesh and set aside. Brush the shells with a little of the olive oil and grill (broil) until soft, about 6–8 minutes. Arrange the shells on a baking sheet and set aside.

Heat the remaining olive oil in a heavy saucepan over a low-medium heat and fry the pork for 3–4 minutes, until browned. Add the onion, garlic and thyme and cook for a further 2 minutes. Add the tomatoes, tomato purée (paste), paprika, cinnamon, wine and the reserved chopped aubergine. Stir in the flour and cook for about 8–10 minutes, until all the liquid has evaporated and the mixture is dry.

Fill the aubergine shells with the stuffing mixture and top each with grated Manchego, breadcrumbs, a drizzle of olive oil and a little paprika. Bake in the oven for 10–15 minutes, until the cheese has melted and the breadcrumbs are golden brown. Serve immediately.

IBERIAN MEATBALLS *with* SPICED PUMPKIN *and* CHICKPEA STEW

Cooking time: 35 minutes
Preparation time: 30 minutes, plus chilling
Serves 4

--- FOR THE MEATBALLS:
450g/1lb minced (ground) pork shoulder
2 tsp cumin seeds
50g/1¾oz/½ cup ground almonds
2 garlic cloves, crushed
2 tbsp chopped flat-leaf parsley
olive oil, for frying
sea salt and freshly ground black pepper

--- FOR THE SPICED PUMPKIN AND CHICKPEA STEW:
2 tbsp olive oil
1 large onion, coarsely chopped
2 garlic cloves, crushed
1 red chilli, deseeded and finely chopped
1 tbsp finely chopped root ginger
1 tsp ground cumin
½ tsp paprika
½ tsp crushed fennel seeds
1 star anise
1 large pinch saffron strands
600g/1lb 5oz pumpkin, peeled and diced
4 tomatoes, peeled, deseeded and diced
1 tsp harissa paste
250ml/9fl oz/1 cup chicken stock (bouillon)
300g/10½oz cooked canned chickpeas
    (garbanzo beans)
1 tbsp chopped fresh coriander (cilantro)
sea salt and freshly ground black pepper

To make the meatballs, thoroughly mix the pork, cumin seeds, ground almonds, garlic and parsley in a large bowl, season with salt and pepper, then shape into 4cm/1½in balls. Chill for at least 30 minutes.

Heat a little olive oil in a frying pan (skillet) over a medium heat. Fry the meatballs for 4–5 minutes, turning from time to time, until golden brown and cooked through. Keep warm.

For the spiced pumpkin and chickpea stew, heat the olive oil in a heavy saucepan over a low-medium heat and add the onions, garlic, chilli, ginger and spices. Stir to combine, cover and cook gently for 2–3 minutes until soft. Add the diced pumpkin, tomatoes, harissa paste and chicken stock (bouillon), season with salt and pepper, and simmer, covered, for 20 minutes.

Add the chickpeas and meatballs to the stew and simmer for a further 5 minutes.

Adjust the seasoning if necessary and sprinkle with chopped coriander (cilantro) to serve.

SOBRASADA *and* ROSEMARY-CRUSTED PORK *with* SAFFRON-APPLE COMPOTE

Cooking time: 55 minutes
Preparation time: 20 minutes
Serves 4–6

750g/1lb 10oz pork loin, trimmed
60ml/2fl oz/¼ cup olive oil
4 garlic cloves, crushed
1 small sprig rosemary
sea salt and freshly ground black pepper

--- FOR THE *SOBRASADA* AND ROSEMARY CRUST:
60g/2oz *sobrasada*
1 garlic clove, crushed
1 sprig rosemary, finely chopped
1½ tsp Dijon mustard
2 tbsp olive oil
50g/1¾oz/1 cup breadcrumbs
sea salt and freshly ground black pepper

--- FOR THE SAFFRON-APPLE COMPOTE:
2 tbsp olive oil
2 large shallots, finely chopped
2 cm/1 in piece of root ginger, peeled and finely chopped
1 garlic clove, finely chopped
4 red apples, peeled and chopped
1 large pinch saffron strands
80g/3oz/scant ½ cup caster (superfine) sugar
2 tbsp cider vinegar
sea salt and freshly ground black pepper

If you can't find sobrasada (see page 49) for this recipe, cooking chorizo is a good alternative, or even 'nduja from Calabria. This is lovely served with puréed potatoes or celeriac (celery root).

To make the *sobrasada* and rosemary crust, combine all of the ingredients for the crust in a food processor and pulse several times to form a smooth mixture. Season with salt and pepper and set aside.

Preheat the oven to 180°C/350°F/gas mark 4.

Season the pork loin well with salt and pepper. Heat a little of the olive oil in a large frying pan (skillet) over a medium heat and sear the meat on all sides until coloured. Transfer the pork to a roasting pan with the garlic cloves and rosemary sprig. Drizzle with the remaining olive oil and roast in the oven for 20 minutes.

Meanwhile, make the compote. Heat the olive oil in a saucepan over a low heat, add the shallots, ginger and garlic and cook for 2–3 minutes, until softened but not coloured. Add the apples,

saffron, sugar and cider vinegar, cover with a lid and gently cook for 15–20 minutes, until thick and syrupy. Season to taste, mix well, remove from the heat and set aside.

Remove the roasting pan from the oven and cover the top of the pork with the *sobrasada* and rosemary crust, pushing down with your fingers to create an even coating. Turn the oven down to 160°C/325°F/gas mark 3 and roast for another 20 minutes, until the pork is still slightly pink in the middle. Remove from the oven, transfer to a cooling rack and let the pork rest for at least 10 minutes before carving.

BRAISED PIGS' CHEEKS *with* BLACK OLIVES *and* SUN-DRIED TOMATOES

Cooking time: 3 hours 10 minutes
Preparation time: 20 minutes, plus
6–8 hours or overnight marinating
Serves 6

12 pigs' cheeks, trimmed
100ml/3½fl oz/scant ½ cup olive oil
100g/3½oz/¾ cup plain (all-purpose) flour
2 tbsp tomato purée (paste)
1l/35fl oz/4¼ cups beef stock (bouillon)
125g/4½oz sun-dried tomatoes, chopped
20 black olives, pitted
10 basil leaves, torn
mashed potatoes or boiled rice, to serve
sea salt and freshly ground black pepper

--- FOR THE MARINADE:
500ml/17fl oz/2 cups red wine
1 large onion, coarsely chopped
3 garlic cloves, crushed
2 carrots, chopped
1 sprig fresh thyme
1 sprig rosemary

At our restaurant, we love to slow-cook delicious, tender pork cheeks until they practically melt in your mouth. They are especially popular during the winter months when there is a little chill in the air. I would argue that stewing and braising are the quintessence of good home cooking. Rich comfort food with robust flavours, cooked slowly in the shape of pot-roasts, casseroles, hot pots and stews, create memorable dishes that are not only delicious but also economical. The addition of black olives, sun-dried tomatoes and basil here give this dish a delicious Mediterranean flavour.

Place the pigs' cheeks in a large bowl and add all the ingredients for the marinade. Mix until the meat is coated, then cover and marinate for 6–8 hours or overnight in the refrigerator.

After marinating, drain the meat (reserving the marinade) and pat dry with paper towels.

Heat the olive oil in a large, heavy saucepan and brown the pigs' cheeks on all sides. Stir in the flour and tomato purée (paste), then add the reserved marinade and pour over the beef stock (bouillon). Cover with a lid and simmer very gently for 3 hours. Use a ladle to remove any fat and impurities that rise to the surface during the cooking.

When ready to serve, add the sun-dried tomatoes, black olives and basil leaves. Season to taste and serve with mashed potatoes or boiled rice.

Lamb
CORDERO

Roast lamb is a magnificent thing, and it never ceases to amaze me how something so simple can be so good. In Mallorca, we even have a "lamb restaurant" that is dedicated to the art. Es Verger is a rustic establishment halfway up the Puig d'Alaró mountain, and it's constantly packed with hungry guests who go on a pilgrimage to eat there. They place a shoulder of sweet spring lamb, a couple of garlic cloves, a sprig of fresh thyme, a splash of white wine and little drizzle of olive oil and seasoning into a wood-burning oven at around 150°C/300°F/gas mark 2. The flavour is bold yet delicate and, as you wait impatiently to tuck in, the aroma of the wood-burning oven is unbelievably tantalizing.

Man has been eating lamb for over 10,000 years, and sheep were probably the first animals domesticated by humans, as we soon discovered that they were not only a good source of food but could also provide wool for our clothing, skins for parchment and milk for butter and cheese. The Spanish are justifiably proud of their lamb, and early spring is probably the best time to enjoy it, when the taste is sweeter and more refined. The local breeds are small and sturdy animals, which lend themselves perfectly to the long, slow cooking favoured by the local restaurants.

At our restaurant, we often serve salt-marsh lamb that graze along the coastline. Their diet of wild grasses and herbs such as sea lavender, fennel and samphire makes them significantly different from the sturdy mountain lambs, giving the meat a distinctive flavour and a meltingly tender texture.

LAMB *PINCHOS MORUÑOS with* CUCUMBER SALAD *and* WALNUT *and* RED PEPPER DIP

Cooking time: 55 minutes
Preparation time: 25 minutes,
plus marinating and chilling
Serves 4 (makes about 16 kebabs)

400g/14oz minced (ground) lamb
   shoulder
2 tbsp finely chopped parsley
200ml/7fl oz/scant 1 cup olive oil,
   plus extra for brushing

--- **FOR THE *MORUÑO* SPICE
MIXTURE:**
2 tsp finely chopped fresh thyme
1 tsp salt
1 tsp ground cumin
1 tsp cayenne pepper
½ tsp black peppercorns
¼ tsp saffron threads
1 bay leaf

--- **FOR THE WALNUT AND RED
PEPPER DIP:**
3 red peppers
80g/3oz/scant ⅔ cup walnuts
60g/2oz/1 cup fresh breadcrumbs
juice of ½ lemon
2 tbsp pomegranate molasses
1 tsp paprika

1 tsp cayenne pepper
½ tsp ground cumin
2 garlic cloves, crushed (optional)
2 tbsp olive oil
sea salt and freshly ground black
   pepper

--- **FOR THE CUCUMBER SALAD:**
1 long cucumber, peeled and diced
2 small red chillies, finely chopped
2 shallots, peeled and finely
   chopped
1 tbsp chopped flat-leaf parsley
1 tbsp granulated sugar
2 tbsp sherry vinegar
juice of 1 lime
6 tbsp olive oil
sea salt and freshly ground black
   pepper

Place all the spice mixture ingredients in a spice grinder or food processor and grind to a coarse powder.

Sprinkle the spice mixture over the minced (ground) lamb, add the chopped parsley and olive oil and mix well. Cover and marinate in the refrigerator for 6–8 hours or overnight.

After marinating, make the dip. Preheat the oven to 200°C/400°F/gas mark 6.

Put the peppers on a baking sheet and roast for 30–35 minutes, turning occasionally, until they are cooked and the skin is blackened. Put the peppers in a bowl, cover with cling film (plastic wrap) and set aside to cool.

When cool enough to handle, peel off and discard the skin and seeds from the peppers, pat the flesh dry and place in a food processor. Add the walnuts, breadcrumbs, lemon juice, molasses, paprika, cayenne, cumin and garlic, if using. Pulse to form a thick paste, then add the olive oil and season to taste. Refrigerate until ready to use.

To make the salad, mix all the ingredients except the seasoning together and refrigerate for 10–15 minutes. Season with salt and pepper just before serving.

When ready to cook, preheat the grill (broiler) to medium or prepare a barbecue for cooking.

Use wet hands to mould the meat into about 16 long sausage shapes, then twist the meat around the skewers, pressing gently all round so that it adheres. Brush each pincho kebab with a little oil and grill (broil) or barbecue for 4–5 minutes on each side, until cooked through.

Serve immediately with the walnut and red pepper dip and marinated cucumber salad.

POMEGRANATE-MARINATED LEG OF LAMB

Cooking time: 1 hour 25 minutes
Preparation time: 10 minutes,
plus marinating and chilling
Serves 4

1 x 1.5kg/3lb 4oz leg of lamb
"*Moro Trampó*" salad (see page
    232), to serve
plain yogurt, to serve

--- **FOR THE MARINADE:**
seeds and juice of ½ pomegranate
1 tbsp pomegranate molasses
100ml/3½fl oz/scant ½ cup dry
    red wine
2 large red onions, halved
juice of 1 lemon
3 garlic cloves
10 black peppercorns, crushed
10 fresh basil leaves
10 fresh mint leaves
6 cumin seeds
1 pinch sea salt

*Pomegranates grow all over our island, and the "**granada**", as it is known in Spain, is steeped in history and romance. The pomegranate is a symbol of fertility and wealth in many countries and a very popular fruit all over the Mediterranean and the Middle East. However, strangely enough, here in Mallorca you rarely see it in any local dishes.*

Here, marinating the lamb in pomegranate, herbs and spices helps to tenderise the meat and makes every bite flavour-packed.

Place the marinade ingredients in a food processor and blend to a paste.

Rub some of the marinade well into the lamb, then place it into a shallow, non-reactive dish. Pour the remaining marinade over the lamb and marinate in the refrigerator for at least 3–4 hours or overnight.

When ready to cook, preheat the oven to 200°C/400°F/gas mark 6.

Wipe off the excess marinade from the meat (reserving it for later) and place the lamb in a roasting pan. Roast for 15 minutes, then reduce the oven temperature to 160°C/325°F/gas mark 3 and roast for a further 1 hour, basting now and again with the reserved marinade.

Rest the lamb for 5–10 minutes before carving. Serve with "*Moro Trampó*" salad and plain yogurt.

ROASTED RACK OF LAMB *in a* FETA, OLIVE *and* ROSEMARY CRUST

Cooking time: 35 minutes
Preparation time: 15 minutes
Serves 4

2 x 550–600g/1lb 3oz–1lb 5oz
    racks of lamb, French-trimmed
1 tbsp olive oil
sea salt and freshly ground black
    pepper
boiled green beans and new
    potatoes, to serve

--- FOR THE FETA, OLIVE AND
ROSEMARY CRUST:
150g/5½oz feta cheese
50g/1¾oz/scant 1 cup fine white
    breadcrumbs
16 green olives, pitted
leaves of 2 fresh rosemary sprigs,
    chopped
handful flat-leaf parsley, roughly
    chopped
4 anchovies in oil, drained
freshly ground black pepper, to
    taste

If you're planning a dinner party to impress, you can't go wrong with this elegant rack of lamb. The flavours of feta, green olives and rosemary give the dish a real kick.

Preheat the oven to 180°C/350°F/gas mark 4.

Cut away the thick layer of fat on the outside of each rack of lamb and season well with salt and pepper. Heat a little olive oil in a large frying pan (skillet) over a medium heat, add the lamb and sear for 2 minutes on each side, until browned all over. Remove and set aside.

To make the crust mixture, place all the ingredients in a food processor and blend to a soft green paste.

Coat the lamb racks with the crust mixture, pressing it on firmly. Put the lamb racks into a large roasting pan and roast for 20 minutes, until the crust is crisp and the meat is still pink.

Set aside to rest for 10 minutes before carving. Serve with green beans and new potatoes.

SAUTÉED MALLORCAN LAMB'S OFFAL

Cooking time: 32 minutes
Preparation time: 20 minutes
Serves 4

150ml/5fl oz/⅔ cup olive oil
2 medium potatoes, peeled and
    diced
3 garlic cloves, crushed
1 aubergine (eggplant), diced
½ bulb fennel, diced
1 red pepper, deseeded and diced
1 green pepper, deseeded and diced
2 bunches spring onions
    (scallions), chopped
1 red chilli, finely chopped
1 tsp paprika
2 bay leaves
1 sprig thyme
350–400g/12–14oz lamb's offal
    (heart, liver and kidney),
    cleaned and diced
10 mint leaves, chopped
sea salt and freshly ground black
    pepper

Frito Mallorquin is a very popular and traditional recipe found in local restaurants all over the island. It is normally made with pork offal, but during the Easter festivities (Pascuas) it is also made with local lamb. It's a rustic, heart-warming dish and full of flavour.

Heat two-thirds of the olive oil in a large, heavy frying pan (skillet) over a medium heat, add the diced potatoes and fry for 10 minutes. Add the garlic, aubergine (eggplant), fennel, peppers, spring onions (scallions), chilli, paprika, bay leaves and thyme and cook for 20 minutes, stirring every few minutes, until the vegetables are cooked and nicely coloured.

Heat the remaining olive oil in a separate frying pan set over a high heat and stir-fry the offal for about 2 minutes, until golden brown. Add the offal to the vegetables and mix well. Add the mint leaves, season to taste and serve immediately.

MEDITERRANEAN SPICED LAMB STEW *with* APRICOTS *and* CORIANDER

Cooking time: 1 hour 45 minutes
Preparation time: 20 minutes,
plus 4 hours marinating
Serves 4

1kg/2lb 3oz lamb shoulder, diced
1 tsp ground cinnamon
1 tsp ground cumin
1 tsp sweet paprika
1 tsp cayenne pepper
100ml/3½fl oz/scant ½ cup olive oil
2 onions, peeled and chopped
2 carrots, peeled and chopped
4 garlic cloves, crushed
1 tsp saffron threads
750ml/26fl oz/3¼ cups chicken
    stock (bouillon)
600g/1lb 5oz canned chopped
    tomatoes
120g/4½oz dried apricots, sliced
1 tsp chopped preserved lemon
1 bunch fresh coriander (cilantro),
    roughly chopped
sea salt and freshly ground black
    pepper

In a large bowl, mix the lamb with the cinnamon, cumin, sweet paprika and cayenne pepper, cover and transfer to the refrigerator to marinate for at least 4 hours, or overnight is ideal.

Warm the olive oil in a large, heavy saucepan over a medium heat, add the marinated lamb and brown on all sides. Add the onions, carrots and garlic and cook gently for 1–2 minutes, then add the saffron threads, stock (bouillon), tomatoes and apricots. Bring slowly to the boil, season with salt and pepper, then cover with a lid, reduce the heat to a gentle simmer and cook for 1½ hours.

Add the chopped preserved lemon and coriander (cilantro), check the seasoning and serve immediately.

Lemons
LIMONES

It's difficult to imagine any kitchen without lemons. There is no other ingredient that can transform a dish in a single squeeze. Choose lemons that are brightly coloured and heavy for their size, with a thin, undamaged skin. Lemons contain an excellent amount of vitamin C, lots of sharp, acidic juice, and also a fragrant oil that's found in the zest.

We are lucky enough to have a few big lemon trees in our vegetable garden and every year we have an abundance of lemons to cook with. We always preserve some in salt to use throughout the year and they make nice culinary gifts for our guests. Known in Morocco as *l'hamd marakad* (sleeping lemons), many Middle Eastern recipes call for preserved lemons, but they are also the perfect condiment for all types of sauces, vinaigrettes and salad dressings. The flavour is soft, yet intensely lemony, with none of the nose-tickling, bright high notes of the fresh lemon. Preserving lemons is also very easy to do at home, although it does take at least three or four weeks before they are ready to use.

PRESERVED
LEMONS

Cooking time: less than 5 minutes
Preparation time: 10 minutes, plus
at least 3 weeks preserving time
Makes 2 x 500ml/17fl oz jars

10 lemons
500ml/17fl oz/2 cups water
325g/11½oz/generous 1½ cups
   coarse sea salt

Bring the water and 275g/10oz/
generous 1¼ cups of the salt
to the boil in a saucepan, then
remove from the heat.

Slice the lemons into quarters
lengthwise, stopping just short
of the stem end, so that the
quarters remain attached at
the base. Rub the lemons in the
remaining salt, then tightly pack
into sterilised jars. Pour the salt
water over the lemons and set
aside to cool.

When cool, cover with a tight-
fitting lid. Store in a cool, dark
place for at least 3 weeks,
upending the jars occasionally
to redistribute the salt, and
topping up the brine if the
lemons become exposed. Once
the lemon peel is soft and ready
to use, move the jars to the
refrigerator. Unopened, the
preserved lemons will keep for
at least 1 year. Once opened,
keep re-covering with salt water
or a layer of olive oil after each
use, and the lemons will keep for
at least 2–3 months.

MARINATED SEA BASS *with* ROASTED PEPPER *and* PRESERVED LEMON SALAD

Cooking time: 15–20 minutes
Preparation time: 15 minutes,
plus 3 hours marinating
Serves 4

1 x 400g/14oz sea bass fillet,
    skinned and deboned
20g/¾oz/4 tsp sea salt
20g/¾oz/5 tsp granulated sugar
grated zest of ½ lemon
4 peppercorns, crushed
few basil or mint leaves, to garnish
olive oil, for drizzling

--- FOR THE ROASTED PEPPER AND
PRESERVED LEMON SALAD:
2 red peppers
2 yellow peppers
2 tbsp culinary argan oil
1 tbsp chopped preserved lemon
    (see page 88)
2 tbsp capers
2 tbsp chopped fresh coriander
    (cilantro)
1 tsp toasted sesame seeds
sea salt and freshly ground black
    pepper

I absolutely adore the combination of roasted peppers and preserved lemons with capers and argan oil. There's something very special about argan oil. It comes from the nuts of the argan tree (Argania spinosa), which grows only in the south-western part of Morocco. It's unusual in cooking, but can be drizzled over food before serving or stirred into soups, couscous and tagines, adding a unique, nutty flavour.

Place the sea bass in a shallow, non-reactive dish. In a small bowl, mix together the salt, sugar, lemon zest and crushed peppercorns, then sprinkle the mixture over the sea bass, pressing down lightly. Cover with cling film (plastic wrap) and marinate in the refrigerator for 3 hours.

Meanwhile, make the salad. Preheat the oven to 200°C/400°F/gas mark 6 or heat the grill (broiler) to hot.

Place the peppers on a baking sheet and roast in the oven or grill (broil) until the skin starts to blacken and blister, about 15–20 minutes. Transfer the peppers to a bowl and cover with cling film (plastic wrap). When cool enough to handle, peel the skin off the peppers, remove the seeds and cut them into thick strips.

Place the peppers in a large bowl, add the remaining salad ingredients and mix to combine. Season to taste, then chill until required.

When ready to serve, rinse the marinade from the sea bass under cold running water, dry well and cut into thin slices. Divide the salad among 4 serving plates and cover with slices of marinated sea bass. Garnish with a few basil or mint leaves, drizzle with olive oil and serve.

GRILLED MACKEREL *with* LEMON, SAMPHIRE *and* A TOMATO *and* CAPER SALSA

Cooking time: 5–10 minutes
Preparation time: 10 minutes
Serves 4

4 x 300g/10½oz fresh mackerel,
    cleaned
olive oil, for brushing
300g/10½oz samphire, washed
    and trimmed
lemon wedges, to serve
sea salt and freshly ground black
    pepper

--- **FOR THE TOMATO AND CAPER SALSA:**
300g/10½oz cherry tomatoes,
    halved
3 tbsp olive oil
1 large garlic clove, thinly sliced
3 tbsp capers
juice of 1 lemon
sea salt and freshly ground black
    pepper

Sea vegetables, packed with iron, calcium, iodine and vitamins, might be fashionable right now, but archaeologists claim that they have been eaten in Asia for about 10,000 years. Sometimes known as 'poor man's asparagus' or 'sea asparagus', samphire – or salicornia as it is known here in Spain – grows abundantly on the shorelines of Mallorca. It has a crisp texture and tastes of the sea. It is particularly useful for vegetarians and vegans who want that seafood taste without the animal ingredients.

To make the salsa, toss the cherry tomatoes in a bowl with the olive oil, garlic, capers and lemon juice and season with salt and pepper. Set aside.

Preheat the grill (broiler) to high or heat a griddle (grill) pan over a high heat.

Score the mackerel on both sides at 2cm/¾in intervals, almost down to the bone. Brush them with olive oil and season with salt and pepper. Grill for 6–7 minutes, turning once, until lightly charred and cooked through.

Meanwhile, bring a saucepan of water to the boil, add the samphire and cook for 1 minute, then drain.

Transfer the grilled mackerel to serving plates, top with the salsa and serve with the samphire and lemon wedges.

LEMON CHICKEN *with* MARJORAM *and* ARTICHOKES

Cooking time: 40–45 minutes
Preparation time: 25 minutes
Serves 4

4 chicken legs, separated into
    drumsticks and thighs
2 tbsp plain (all-purpose) flour
2 tbsp olive oil
2 onions, finely chopped
1 garlic clove, crushed
1 tsp paprika
1 bay leaf
100ml/3½fl oz/scant ½ cup white
    wine
2 tbsp sherry vinegar
250ml/9fl oz/1 cup chicken stock
    (bouillon)
2 large globe artichokes, cooked
    (see page 248) and quartered
2 tbsp chopped marjoram
juice of 2 lemons
1 tbsp chopped flat-leaf parsley
sea salt and freshly ground black
    pepper

Dust the chicken pieces very lightly with flour and season with salt and pepper.

Heat the olive oil in a large, heavy saucepan over a high heat, add the chicken and cook over a high heat for 5–6 minutes, turning frequently, until a golden crust has formed. Reduce the heat and add the onions, garlic, paprika and the bay leaf and cook for 3–4 minutes, until the onions are softened but not coloured.

Add the white wine and sherry vinegar, allowing the wine to bubble and reduce for 1–2 minutes, then add the chicken stock (bouillon). Cover the pan with a lid and cook over a low heat for about 30 minutes, stirring halfway through.

Just before serving, stir through the cooked artichokes, marjoram and lemon juice. Season to taste, sprinkle with chopped parsley and serve immediately.

MEDITERRANEAN SPICES

I love the smell of gently toasted spices and the way they fill the kitchen with the most amazing aromas. The sheer variety of flavours that they have to offer is endless, but seasoning with herbs and spices means complementing your dishes, not overwhelming them and hiding the true flavour of the food.

Mediterranean cooks have been blending spices for centuries, and they were among the first of many foods brought back to Europe from the East by Marco Polo. Indeed, the spice trade encouraged the early voyages of Columbus and Vasco da Gama. Today, when spices cost so little and we can all enjoy freshly ground black pepper and the delicious aromas of cinnamon, ginger, cardamom and cloves with ease, it's hard to believe that these fragrant bits of bark, leaves and

seeds were once so costly, and so hard to track down and transport, that men were willing to risk their lives crossing oceans and waging wars in an attempt to bring them back. Empires were built with the profits from the resulting spice trade.

Ras el hanout is a great spice mixture to have kicking around your kitchen. It literally means "head of the shop", meaning the very best a spice merchant has to offer. This complex medley of seasonings is notable for its rich aroma and well-balanced, curry-like flavour. The mixture occasionally has up to 100 different spices and is extremely popular throughout Morocco and the rest of the Middle East. It allegedly promotes a sense of wellbeing and enhances sexual vigour ... so give this recipe a try!

RAS EL HANOUT

Cooking time: 1 minute
Preparation time: 5 minutes
Makes 1 x 70g/2½oz jar

Don't be put off by the number of ingredients – this really is a doddle to make. It keeps well in a jar and can be used in so many dishes.

2 tsp black peppercorns
2 tsp fennel seeds
4 tsp coriander seeds
16 cardamom pods
2 tsp yellow mustard seeds
4 tsp cumin seeds
1 cinnamon stick
½ tsp freshly grated nutmeg
1 tsp cayenne pepper
2 tsp turmeric
2 tsp paprika
1 tsp sea salt

In a hot, dry frying pan (skillet), gently toast the peppercorns, fennel, coriander seeds, cardamom pods, mustard seeds, cumin and the cinnamon stick until fragrant, about 30 seconds–1 minute, then add the remaining ingredients and grind to a fine powder. Store in an airtight container.

PRESERVED LEMON CREAM *with* PISTACHIO DUKKAH, CHERRY-ROSEWATER SORBET *and* RAS EL HANOUT CARAMEL SAUCE

Cooking time: 15 minutes
Preparation time: 30 minutes, plus chilling/infusing
Serves 6–8

This is another signature dessert from the restaurant. I always say that it's a great dish for people who don't normally like desserts, because the flavour profiles are so interesting. When I came up with the idea for this dish, I thought it would be stimulating and slightly challenging to incorporate preserved lemons into a dessert. I then decided to introduce other Middle Eastern elements that are normally associated with savoury recipes, such as dukkah, rosewater and ras el hanout (see page 97).

Dukkah is one of my culinary obsessions. It is an Egyptian side dish consisting of a mixture of nuts (usually hazelnut, although my favourite is with pistachios) and spices that are lightly toasted and then crushed. When still warm, the aroma is amazing. The name dukkah actually means, "to crush" or "to pound" in Arabic. It is typically used as a dip with bread and olive oil and it also makes a perfect crust for lamb or chicken.

This dessert has become a firm favourite with our guests, and although it's very unusual, it's also utterly delicious!

--- **FOR THE PRESERVED LEMON CREAM:**
7 medium egg yolks
125g/4½oz/scant ⅔ cup caster (superfine) sugar
3 tbsp plain (all-purpose) flour
1 tsp cornflour (cornstarch)
400ml/14fl oz/1 ⅔ cups milk

100ml/3½fl oz/scant ½ cup double
(heavy) cream
1 vanilla pod
juice of 1 lemon
1–2 tsp finely chopped preserved
lemons (see page 88)

--- FOR THE RAS EL HANOUT
CARAMEL SAUCE:
100ml/3½fl oz/scant ½ cup water
225g/8oz/scant 1¼ cups caster
(superfine) sugar
80g/3oz/¾ stick unsalted butter
2 tbsp double (heavy) cream
1 tsp ras el hanout (see page 97)

--- FOR THE CHERRY-ROSEWATER
SORBET:
180g/6¼oz/1⅓ cups caster
(superfine) sugar
250ml/9fl oz/1 cup water
juice of ½ lemon
450g/1lb fresh cherries, pitted
1 tsp rosewater syrup

--- FOR THE PISTACHIO DUKKAH:
120g/4½oz green pistachios,
peeled
4 tbsp sesame seeds
2 tbsp coriander seeds
1 tbsp cumin seeds
1 tbsp fennel seeds
sea salt and freshly ground black
pepper, to taste

To make the preserved lemon cream, whisk the egg yolks and sugar together in a large bowl until light and fluffy. Stir the flour and cornflour (cornstarch) until well combined.

Bring the milk, cream and vanilla pod to the boil in a heavy saucepan, then reduce the heat and simmer for about 2 minutes. Remove the pan from the heat and pour the hot milk into the egg mixture, whisking continuously, then return the mixture to the pan.

Place the pan over a low heat and cook for about 4–5 minutes, whisking continuously, until the cream starts to thicken. Remove from the heat and add the lemon juice and preserved lemons. Leave to cool and infuse for 15 minutes, then pass through a fine sieve (strainer) into a bowl, cover with cling film (plastic wrap) and chill in the refrigerator for at least 4 hours.

To make the ras el hanout caramel sauce, bring the water and sugar to the boil in a heavy saucepan. Cook until the caramel reaches a golden brown, about 3–4 minutes. Remove from the heat and carefully add the butter and cream, whisking continuously. Stir in the ras el hanout, then pass the mixture through a fine sieve (strainer). Chill until required.

For the cherry-rosewater sorbet, bring all the ingredients to the boil in a large saucepan. Transfer to a blender or food processor and blend to a purée, then pass the mixture through a fine sieve (strainer). Churn in an ice cream machine (according to the manufacturer's directions) until smooth. Store in an airtight container in the freezer until required.

To make the pistachio dukkah, heat the oven to 180°C/350°F/ gas mark 4. Lightly roast the nuts and seeds on a baking sheet in the oven for about 1 minute, until they begin to colour and release their aroma. Crush in a pestle and mortar or place in a food processor and grind to a coarse mixture. Finish with a little seasoning. Store in an airtight container.

To serve, place 2–3 tablespoons of the preserved lemon cream into dessert bowls and sprinkle the entire surface with pistachio dukkah. Add a spoonful of cherry-rosewater sorbet and finish with a little ras el hanout caramel sauce.

LEMON and CREAM CHEESE TARTLETS with RED FRUITS

Cooking time: 30–40 minutes
Preparation time: 25 minutes,
plus chilling
Makes 10 tartlets

4 eggs
250g/9oz/1¼ cups caster
    (superfine) sugar
300g/10½oz/1¼ cups requesón
    or cream cheese
50ml/2fl oz/¼ cup double (heavy)
    cream
1 pinch ground cinnamon
grated zest of 1 lemon
juice of 2 lemons
icing (confectioners') sugar, for
    dusting
450g/1lb red fruits (raspberries,
    strawberries, blueberries, etc.),
    to decorate

--- FOR THE SWEET PASTRY:
200g/7oz/1¾ sticks cold unsalted
    butter, diced, plus extra for
    greasing
450g/1lb/scant 3½ cups plain (all-
    purpose) flour
1 pinch salt
150g/5¼oz/1¼ cups icing
    (confectioners') sugar
3 egg yolks

Most Spanish pastelarias (bakeries) sell these little pastry tarts known as tarta de Requesón (Requesón is a Spanish cream cheese that's very similar to ricotta). They make a perfect breakfast snack with a café con leche, or a great, simple dessert with red fruits and a scoop of vanilla ice cream. I like to add a little extra citrus kick with the addition of the grated zest and juice of fresh lemons. Be warned, these little tartlets are extremely tempting!

To make the sweet pastry, place the butter, flour and salt in a food processor and pulse until it resembles breadcrumbs. Add the icing (confectioners') sugar and egg yolks and pulse again, just enough to incorporate the eggs. Scrape out the pastry, wrap in clingfilm (plastic wrap) and chill in the refrigerator for at least 30 minutes.

Lightly grease 10 x 7.5cm/3in individual tart pans.

Roll out the chilled pastry to a thickness of 5mm/¼in. Cut out circles with a pastry cutter

and line the tart pans with the pastry. Chill in the refrigerator for at least 30 minutes.

Preheat the oven to 200°C/400°F/gas mark 6.

Cover the base of the pastry cases with baking parchment or foil and fill with a few baking beans (pie weights). Blind bake the pastry cases for 7 minutes, then remove the parchment and beans. Return the pastry cases to the oven for a further 4–5 minutes, or until light golden-brown and completely dry.

Reduce the oven temperature to 160°C/325°F/gas mark 3.

Break the whole eggs into a bowl, add the sugar and beat until smooth. Add the cream cheese, cream, cinnamon, lemon zest and juice and whisk together until smooth. Pour the mixture into the pastry cases and bake for 20–25 minutes until just set.

Remove from the oven and leave to cool. Dust the tartlets with icing sugar and serve decorated with red fruits.

Mediterranean Herbs
HIERBAS MEDITERRANEAS

I couldn't imagine my kitchen without fresh herbs. A simple dish can be transformed just by using a few fresh herbs, as they greatly enhance the taste, appearance and nutritional value of practically all the food we eat.

The word "herb" comes from the Latin *herba*, meaning "grass" or "green plant" and Mediterranean herbs have played an important part in the region's culture and the wellbeing of its people for thousands of years. Records date back to 2800BC, when the ancient Egyptians used herbs for dyes, perfumes and food. These days we still appreciate herbs for their culinary and medicinal values.

In the kitchen, bland food can be made exciting with the addition of herbs, and they can help to enhance and bring out the natural flavours of food in a similar way to salt. However, it is important to use herbs correctly: too many can overpower and completely overshadow the natural flavour of a dish; too few will achieve nothing. The addition of herbs must be balanced to complement the natural flavours that are already present in foods.

Herbs do deteriorate very quickly once they've been picked. I always advise growing your own small selection of herbs, in pots or a window box if necessary, so they will always be on hand when you need them. Early spring is the perfect time to organise your herb garden. Alongside favourites such as parsley, chervil, tarragon, mint and lemon balm, try planting a few more obscure herbs such as summer savoury, lovage, woodruff, hyssop, borage or rue, to complement the classic sturdy Mediterranean herbs of rosemary, sage, thyme, fennel, marjoram and oregano.

When cooking with herbs, there are a couple of basic rules you need to apply: those with tougher leaves generally have a stronger flavour and are usually added at the start of cooking (e.g. sage, rosemary, thyme or winter savoury). These herbs *can* be added towards the end of cooking, but will need to be very finely chopped and used sparingly. Whole sprigs can be added to soups, stews, casseroles, roasts and marinades, but should be removed before serving. If the plants have soft, lush leaves, add them at the end of cooking, in order to retain their full flavour, colour and nutritional content (e.g. parsley, chervil, chives, basil, mint, coriander and dill). Fresh herbs are much more gentle in flavour than dried, normally requiring twice as much to be used in any recipe. Dried herbs and spices need time to release their flavours and should be added at the beginning of cooking, while fresh are much better added near the end.

To maximize the usefulness of a herb garden, use the fresh herbs to make condiments. Herb vinegars are ideal for salad dressings and used in various sauces such as hollandaise. Simply place fresh herbs in a bottle of vinegar and let it stand, sealed, for at least 2–3 weeks. You can do the same with non-aromatic oils to make aromatic herb oils. Suitable herbs include tarragon, sage, marjoram, rosemary, thyme and savoury. Or how about herb butter? Finely chopped herbs can be mixed with butter and spread over freshly baked bread or to add flavour to roasted tomatoes and boiled vegetables. Herb salts (see page 108) can be really useful as well: mix a little chopped thyme, rosemary, oregano and marjoram with *flor de sal* to make a wonderfully aromatic herbed salt.

BOUQUET GARNI   FLAVOURED SALTS

*One of the first things I was taught to make in the kitchen was a classic **bouquet garni**. This is a bundle of herbs that is added to casseroles, stocks, sauces and soups. It traditionally comprises parsley (or parsley stalks, which have lots of flavour), a few sprigs of thyme and a bay leaf. These herbs may be bundled together with a strip of leek or a piece of celery stalk, or tied with kitchen string, to keep them together during cooking and allow for easy removal before serving.*

--- **FOR 1 *BOUQUET GARNI*:**
2 sprigs thyme
1 large bay leaf
2 parsley stalks

Gather together the thyme, bay leaf and parsley stalks into a small bundle and secure tightly with kitchen string. Use as your recipe requires.

Flavoured salt is sometimes all you need to bring a dish to life. If you have a food processor, making them is easy. You can process dried herbs such as thyme, rosemary, fennel, juniper or lavender with sea salt and use it to flavour anything from grilled fish or fried squid to steaks and lamb cutlets. I recommend using flor de sal for these recipes. Superlative salt has a great capacity to accentuate flavours, and flor de sal has a wonderfully pure, clean, salty taste. Flor de sal (known as fleur de sel in France) is the very first layer of salt that crystallizes on the surface of the salt marshes. It is harvested by a traditional extraction method, is 100 per cent natural and reaches your palate without having suffered any alteration.

--- **MEDITERRANEAN HERB SALT:**
1 tsp dried rosemary
1 tsp dried thyme
1 tsp dried oregano
1 tsp dried sage
1 tsp summer savoury
150g/5½oz/10 tbsp sea salt flakes

In a food processor or blender, pulse the herbs until finely chopped. Add the salt and pulse several times to combine well. Store in an airtight container.

--- **LEMON AND CHILLI SALT:**
2 tbsp grated lemon zest (or orange or lime)
1 dried red chilli
125g/4½oz/8 tbsp sea salt flakes

In a food processor or blender, pulse the lemon zest and chilli until very finely chopped. Add the salt and pulse several times to combine well. Store in an airtight container.

MEDITERRANEAN POTATO *and* HERB SALAD

Cooking time: 10–15 minutes
Preparation time: 15 minutes
Serves 4

900g/2lb new potatoes
sea salt, for the cooking water
1 medium onion, finely chopped
100g/3½oz sun-dried tomatoes,
    chopped
300ml/10½fl oz/1¼ cups olive oil
2 tbsp sherry vinegar
20 black olives, pitted
2 salted anchovy fillets, chopped
15–20 capers
2 tbsp finely chopped chives
2 tbsp chopped fresh coriander
    (cilantro)
6–8 basil leaves, torn
300ml/10½fl oz/1¼ cups
    mayonnaise
freshly ground black pepper,
    to taste

Boil the new potatoes in a large saucepan of salted water until just cooked, about 10–15 minutes. Drain and, while still warm, cut the potatoes in half and place them in a bowl. Add the rest of the ingredients and stir to lightly bind the salad together. Serve immediately.

SALSA VERDE

Cooking time: N/A
Preparation time: 10 minutes
Serves 4

½ small bunch basil
½ small bunch flat-leaf parsley
1 tbsp capers, rinsed and drained
1 tbsp sherry vinegar
1 garlic clove, crushed
1 salted anchovy, rinsed
1 tsp Dijon mustard
150ml/5fl oz/⅔ cup olive oil
sea salt and freshly ground black
    pepper

This classic Mediterranean sauce is rather like chimichurri taken to the next level.

There are so many variations, but if you're going to pick one sauce for your next barbecue, make it this one!

Blend the herbs, capers, vinegar, garlic, anchovy, mustard and olive oil in a food processor to a smooth consistency (add a little water if necessary, to loosen).

Season to taste and serve immediately, or store for up to 3 days in an airtight container in the refrigerator.

ROASTED RIB EYE *with a* HERB *and* GRAIN MUSTARD CRUST

Cooking time: 1 hour 15–20 minutes
Preparation time: 10 minutes
Serves 4–6

2kg/4½lb rib-eye beef steak
drizzle olive oil, for searing
5 sprigs thyme
1 bulb garlic, cloves separated
    but unpeeled and very lightly
    crushed under the blade of a
    knife
sea salt and freshly ground black
    pepper

--- **FOR THE HERB AND GRAIN
MUSTARD CRUST:**
4 slices stale bread
30g/1oz Parmesan, grated
1 bunch flat-leaf parsley
1 sprig thyme
1 sprig rosemary
2 tbsp grain mustard
1 tbsp olive oil
sea salt and freshly ground black
    pepper

A beautiful piece of rib-eye steak, roasted with Mediterranean herbs, mustard and garlic cloves, looks spectacular and tastes even better. I love to serve this with glazed new potatoes and green beans.

To make the crust mixture, place the bread in a food processor and pulse into crumbs, then add the remaining ingredients and pulse several times until well combined. Season with salt and pepper and set aside.

Preheat the oven to 220°C/425°F/gas mark 7.

Season the beef well with salt and pepper. Heat a little oil in a large frying pan (skillet) over a medium heat and sear the beef until coloured on all sides. Transfer the beef to a roasting pan with the thyme sprigs and garlic cloves. Roast in the oven for 30 minutes.

Remove the beef from the oven and cover with the crust mixture. Turn the oven down to 190°C/375°F/gas mark 5. Roast for a further 35 minutes, until medium rare. Remove the beef from the oven, transfer to a cooling rack and let it rest for 10–15 minutes before carving.

HERB-ROASTED GUINEA FOWL *with* COUSCOUS

Cooking time: 1 hour 5 minutes
Preparation time: 20 minutes
Serves 2–3

1 x 1.2kg/2lb 10oz guinea fowl
2 lemons, chopped (with peel)
6 garlic cloves, lightly crushed
2 sprigs rosemary
10 sage leaves, finely chopped
120g/4½oz/generous 1 stick salted
    butter, softened
grated zest of 1 lemon
2 tbsp olive oil
2–3 sprigs thyme
125ml/4fl oz/½ cup dry white wine
200ml/7fl oz/scant 1 cup chicken
    stock (bouillon)
sea salt and freshly ground black
    pepper

--- FOR THE COUSCOUS SALAD:
6 green asparagus spears
200g/7oz/generous 1 cup couscous
½ red onion, finely chopped
1 tbsp chopped flat-leaf parsley
juice of 2 lemons
1 tsp finely chopped rosemary
1 tsp finely chopped lemon thyme
1 tbsp olive oil
200ml/7fl oz/scant 1 cup boiling
    chicken stock (bouillon)
sea salt and freshly ground black
    pepper

*Known as **pintada** in Spain and sometimes called an African pheasant, guinea fowl is similar to chicken, but has a mild gamey flavour. Guinea fowl is unusual in that it is neither totally wild nor truly domesticated, and has been reared for the table since Elizabethan times.*

Preheat the oven to 200°C/400°F/gas mark 6.

Fill the cavity of the guinea fowl with the chopped lemon, garlic cloves and rosemary sprigs. Season well with salt and pepper, then tie the feet together with kitchen string.

Mix the chopped sage with the softened butter, the lemon zest and some seasoning. Push some of the butter under the skin of the guinea fowl, then rub the rest of the butter all over the outside of the bird. Place the bird a roasting pan, season with salt and pepper, drizzle with olive oil and sprinkle with the thyme sprigs. Roast for 30 minutes.

Reduce the oven temparature to 180°C/350°F/gas mark 4. Pour the white wine and chicken stock (bouillon) into the roasting pan and continue roasting for another 25 minutes, until the guinea fowl is golden and tender. To test, pierce the flesh between the thigh and breast; the juices should run clear. Let the guinea fowl rest for 10 minutes before carving.

Meanwhile, blanch the asparagus spears in boiling water for 8 minutes, then drain and set aside.

Place the couscous, red onion, parsley, lemon juice, rosemary, thyme and olive oil into a large bowl and mix together. Pour over the boiling chicken stock (bouillon), cover with cling film (plastic wrap) and allow to steam for 3–4 minutes. Remove the cling film, add the asparagus spears and season with salt and pepper, then mix well using a fork.

Transfer the couscous salad to a serving dish and serve alongside the roasted guinea fowl.

ROSEMARY *and* FENNEL SEED GLAZED DUCK *with* SWEET POTATO RAGOUT *and* FIGS

Cooking time: 30 minutes
Preparation time: 15 minutes
Serves 4

4 duck breasts
6 fresh figs, halved
sea salt and freshly ground black pepper

--- FOR THE GLAZE:
1 tsp fennel seeds
1 tbsp chopped rosemary
150ml/5fl oz/⅔ cup maple syrup
100ml/3½fl oz/scant ½ cup water

--- FOR THE SWEET POTATO RAGOUT:
2 tbsp olive oil
1 onion, chopped
2 garlic cloves, crushed
2 tsp paprika
1 tsp cayenne pepper
1 tsp ground cumin
1 tsp chopped rosemary
600g/1lb 5oz sweet potatoes, peeled and diced
400g/14oz tomatoes, chopped
1 tbsp sherry vinegar
sea salt and freshly ground black pepper

Preheat the oven to 200°C/400°F/gas mark 6.

For the ragout, heat the olive oil in a heavy saucepan over a low-medium heat, add the onions and garlic and sweat until softened. Add the paprika, cayenne pepper, cumin and rosemary and cook for a further 1 minute. Add the sweet potatoes, chopped tomatoes and sherry vinegar and cook, stirring occasionally, for 25 minutes, until the potatoes are cooked through. Season with salt and pepper before serving.

Meanwhile, to make the glaze, lightly toast the fennel seeds in a dry frying pan (skillet). Add the rosemary, maple syrup and water and bring to the boil. Simmer until reduced to a light syrup, about 2 minutes. Remove from the heat and set aside.

Season the duck breasts with salt and pepper. Heat a separate heavy frying pan over a medium heat. Place the duck breasts in the pan, skin-side down, and fry gently until crisp and golden, about 3–4 minutes. Transfer

the duck breasts to a baking sheet, skin-side up. Using a pastry brush, coat the skin with the glaze mixture. Roast in the oven for 4–6 minutes, until just cooked and pink in the middle. Remove from the oven and set aside to rest in a warm place for 2–3 minutes.

Serve the glazed duck with the sweet potato ragout and the fresh figs alongside.

Mussels
MEJILLONES

In my opinion, fresh mussels offer up a complete sensory food experience. For a start, they look really cool in their elegant, shiny black shells. Then, there's the clattering sound of them being gently shaken in the pan and poured into a large bowl, and finally you get to breathe in that amazing sea-fresh aroma before extracting the succulent mussels from their shells and enjoying all their wonderful, gutsy flavour. If that wasn't enough, the best is still to come. After cooking, you are left with an intensely rich, tantalizing broth that offers up the most incredible taste sensation. As you soak up that delicious, fragrant broth with pieces of crusty bread, you come to the realization that nothing else tastes quite the same.

Often regarded as the poor man's shellfish, mussels are cheap, plentiful and entirely sustainable. Archaeological findings suggest that mussels have been used as a food for over 20,000 years. They are a good source of vitamin B12, zinc, folic acid and omega 3.

Spanish mussels, along with clams, appear in just about every seafood dish you care to imagine, from the ubiquitous *paella* to the various fish soups, stews and *calderetas* all along Spain's vast coastline. In the sheltered bays of the Spanish Atlantic coast, mussels are commercially grown, hanging from ropes attached to stakes in mussel farms. The constant exchange of water through the ebb and flow of the tides encourages the build-up of plankton, the mussels' main food source. Today, there are over 3,000 firmly anchored floats along the coast of Galicia alone, from which the mussel-covered ropes are suspended. The ropes, which can weigh over 115kg/250lb, are hauled into boats and stripped of their harvest.

As mussels tend to live in shallow, sandy waters, they take grit and other particles into their shells when they feed. A good way to purge fresh mussels of this grit is to place them in a bucket of cold, salted water with an added sprinkling of oatmeal or flour. The shellfish will feed on the oatmeal and excrete the dirt. To prepare them for cooking, wash the mussel shells thoroughly, using a scrubbing brush to remove any barnacles along with their "beards" (the hairy-looking filaments that adhere their shells to the rocks). Discard any mussels that are not tightly closed or have broken shells. Give them a little tap on the tabletop to see if they close.

SUQUET DE PEIX

Cooking time: 25–30 minutes
Preparation time: 25 minutes
Serves 6

200ml/7fl oz/scant 1 cup olive oil
1 onion (preferably Spanish),
    chopped
4 garlic cloves
4 tomatoes, peeled and chopped
2 potatoes, peeled and sliced
1 pinch saffron threads
1.2l/40fl oz/5 cups fish stock
    (bouillon)
250g/9oz monkfish tail, filleted
    and cut into bite-size pieces
250g/9oz sea bream fillets, cut
    into bite-size pieces
700g/1lb 9oz fresh mussels,
    cleaned and de-bearded
100g/3½oz toasted almonds,
    ground
1 tbsp chopped flat-leaf parsley
sea salt and freshly ground black
    pepper

The fishing villages all along the Spanish coastline are famous for their popular fish stews and soups. These include some truly wonderful dishes, such as calder`eta, zarzuela and suquet de peix. A Catalan suquet is just about my favourite thing to eat. It is, quite simply, a meal in itself – needing only a little crusty bread and maybe a nice crisp dry white wine for company. Here in the Balearic Islands, the local markets always have a selection of weird and wonderful tiny rockfish that are grouped together and called **moralla.** *These tasty little rockfish are perfect for flavouring robust fish soups and stocks (bouillon), but any combination of fresh fish can be used.*

Heat the olive oil in a heavy saucepan over a low-medium heat, add the onions and cook until softened, about 2–3 minutes. Add the garlic, tomatoes, potatoes and saffron, then cover with fish stock (bouillon) and bring to the boil. Reduce the heat to a simmer and cook for 10–15 minutes, until the potatoes are tender.

Stir in the fish, mussels (ensuring they are all tightly closed) and toasted ground almonds and cook for another 10 minutes, until all the mussels have opened (discard any that have remained closed) and the fish is cooked through. Add the chopped parsley and season to taste. Pour into a soup tureen and serve immediately.

FRESH MUSSEL
ESCABECHE

Cooking time: 10–15 minutes
Preparation time: 15 minutes,
plus 24 hours chilling
Serves 4

1kg/2lb 3oz fresh mussels, cleaned
    and de-bearded
sea salt, for the cooking water
fresh olives and salad leaves,
    to serve

--- **FOR THE *ESCABECHE*:**
250ml/9fl oz/1 cup olive oil
120ml/4fl oz/½ cup sherry vinegar
125ml/4fl oz/½ cup water
100ml/3½fl oz/scant ½ cup dry
    white wine
5 black peppercorns, crushed
1 small onion, thinly sliced into
    rings
4 garlic cloves, crushed
1 tsp paprika
1 tsp dried oregano
1 clove
2 bay leaves
1 tsp sea salt

"Escabeche" pickling has been a common practice for preserving food in Spain for over a thousand years. Using a stock (bouillon) made of vinegar, wine, oil, bay leaves and peppercorns, many types of foods are pickled in this way, from wild mushrooms to small game birds to all types of seafood. Escabeche of mussels can be made the day before and is a perfect appetiser as part of a tapas platter. It's quick, easy and inexpensive to make and is also delicious.

Place all the ingredients for the *escabeche* in a heavy saucepan over a low-medium heat and cook slowly for 10–15 minutes.

Meanwhile, bring a saucepan of salted water to the boil and blanch the mussels (ensuring they are all tightly closed) until they open, about 2 minutes. Do this in batches, if necessary, and discard any mussels that have remained closed. Drain and let cool slightly.

As soon as they are cool enough to handle, remove the mussels from their shells and add them to the *escabeche* mixture. Remove from the heat and leave to cool completely. When cool, chill in the refrigerator for at least 24 hours.

Serve with fresh olives and salad leaves.

SPANISH-STYLE MUSSELS *with* OLIVES, CHORIZO *and* SHERRY

Cooking time: 8–10 minutes
Preparation time: 10 minutes
Serves 4

2 tbsp olive oil
1 onion, finely chopped
50g/1¾oz chorizo, diced
½ red pepper, finely chopped
4 garlic cloves, crushed
1.25kg/2lb 12oz fresh mussels,
    cleaned and de-bearded
150ml/5fl oz/⅔ cup dry (fino)
    sherry
24 green olives (preferably
    manzanillas), finely chopped
3 tomatoes, peeled and diced
juice of 1 lemon
2 tbsp finely chopped flat-leaf
    parsley
sea salt and freshly ground black
    pepper

All Spanish flavours seem to marry well with mussels. This is one of my favourite recipes, and whenever I'm looking for a simple, delicious supper dish to share with family and friends, it never lets me down.

Heat the olive oil in a large saucepan over a low heat, add the onion, chorizo, red pepper and garlic and cook for 2–3 minutes, stirring until softened. Stir in the mussels (ensuring they are all tightly closed) until they are evenly coated in the peppery mixture, then add the sherry, cover with a lid and steam for 4–5 minutes, until the mussels are just starting to open.

Add the olives, tomatoes, lemon juice and parsley, season with salt and pepper and stir briefly to combine, then cover again with the lid and cook for a further 1 minute. Bring the pan to the table, remove the lid and serve immediately. Remember to discard any mussels that have remained closed after cooking.

BAKED MUSSELS *with* TOMATO, PARMESAN *and* BASIL

Cooking time: 15–19 minutes
Preparation time: 15 minutes
Serves 4

4 tbsp olive oil
1 medium onion, finely chopped
2 garlic cloves, chopped
½ tsp paprika
juice of ½ lemon
200ml/7fl oz/scant 1 cup dry white wine
1kg/2lb 3oz fresh mussels, cleaned and de-bearded
200ml/7fl oz/scant 1 cup fresh tomato sauce
10 basil leaves, torn
2 tbsp finely chopped flat-leaf parsley
1 pinch flor de sal
50g/1¾oz Parmesan, grated
50g/1¾oz/1 cup white breadcrumbs
crusty bread, to serve

Preheat the oven to 180°C/350°F/gas mark 4.

Heat the olive oil in a large saucepan over a low-medium heat, add the onion and garlic and sweat until softened, about 2–3 minutes. Add the paprika, lemon juice, dry white wine and mussels (ensuring they are all tightly closed), cover with a lid and gently cook for about 5–6 minutes, until all the mussels have opened.

Remove from the heat, discard any mussels that have remained closed and strain the cooking liquid into a clean saucepan. When cool enough to handle, remove the mussels from their shells, reserving half of each mussel shell. Place the reserved mussel shells on a baking sheet.

Bring the cooking liquid to the boil and add the fresh tomato sauce. Reduce the heat and cook for a further 3–4 minutes, until the sauce is thickened, then stir in the basil, parsley, *flor de sal* and cooked mussels.

Spoon the mussels and sauce back into the empty shells (1 per shell), sprinkle over the Parmesan and breadcrumbs and bake in the oven for 4–5 minutes, or until golden brown and bubbling on top. Serve with crusty white bread.

MONKFISH TAILS *with* MUSSELS, SAFFRON, CIDER *and* LEEKS

Cooking time: 25–30 minutes
Preparation time: 20 minutes
Serves 4

4 tbsp olive oil
4 x 220g/8oz monkfish tails
1 onion, finely chopped
2 leeks, cleaned and chopped
4 garlic cloves, finely chopped
½ tsp saffron
½ tsp paprika
250g/9oz tomatoes, peeled, deseeded and chopped
350ml/12fl oz/1½ cups dry cider
300ml/10½fl oz/1¼ cups fish stock (bouillon)
400g/14oz fresh mussels, cleaned and de-bearded
2 tbsp finely chopped chives
sea salt and freshly ground black pepper

Heat the olive oil in a large, heavy saucepan over a low-medium heat, add the monkfish and sear for 1–2 minutes on each side, then remove and set aside.

Add the onion, leeks, garlic, saffron and paprika to the same pan and cook for 2–3 minutes, stirring until softened. Add the tomatoes, cider and fish stock (bouillon) and cook for 15–20 minutes, stirring occasionally, until the sauce has thickened.

Add the mussels (ensuring they are all tightly closed) and monkfish, cover with a lid and cook for 5 minutes, until all the mussels are open (discard any that have remained closed). Season to taste, sprinkle with chopped chives and serve immediately.

Olive Oil
ACEITE DE OLIVA

We are extremely fortunate to have a friend who supplies our olive oil at the restaurant, and it arrives freshly pressed every week, with a truly amazing, fruity aroma. Pep Solivellas is one of Mallorca's true, unassuming food heroes. He went from managing a local bank to producing some of the best extra virgin olive oils that I have tasted anywhere. Working alongside his family at his Es Guinyent estate, near the village of Pollença, Pep is at his happiest sitting on his tractor, smoking a big fat cigar and fussing over his olive trees. While I'm wandering around the olive groves listening to Pep wax lyrical about the many benefits of olive oil, I can't help thinking about how things have changed over the past forty years. When I was just a kid, growing up on the outskirts of London in the sixties and seventies, the only place you could buy olive oil was in a chemist or pharmacy! It was sold in tiny bottles and used to treat ear problems, but it was never really used in cooking. When I first became a professional chef in the early eighties, I was schooled in classic French techniques, where cream and butter were omnipresent and olive oil would only occasionally make a brief appearance in vinaigrettes or salad dressings. Luckily, things have changed, as I couldn't imagine my kitchen now without it.

In the Mediterranean region, we are blessed with a staggering 93 per cent of the approximately 800 million olive trees in the world. The humble olive has the distinction of being the oldest tree in cultivation in the Western Hemisphere, has been the subject of mythology and is a sign of longevity.

Its oil has annointed kings, polished finely cut diamonds and been used in medicinal balms and the manufacture of soaps. When I first moved to Spain, I still remember the day that my attitude towards olive oil changed forever. I was in the beautiful Basque city of San Sebastian watching a chef preparing a classic, salt cod dish known as bacalao al pil-pil (see also page xxx). I was fascinated as he poured half a litre of olive oil into an earthenware dish and cooked a few slices of garlic and a little chilli over a gentle flame before adding four or five fillets of salted cod. When the cod was almost cooked, he removed the dish from the heat and started making circular motions with the dish, slowly emulsifying the olive oil with the natural gelatine from the fish. In about five minutes he had a delicious, silky smooth white sauce coating the fish almost like a hollandaise and, as soon as I tasted that dish, my love of olive oil truly began in earnest. How could two very basic ingredients, cod and olive oil, produce such a sophisticated and delicious dish? In that moment, my cooking philosophy changed, and I slowly started to develop my own style of cooking, with good-quality olive oil as one of my indispensible ingredients.

Olive oil is judged by its acidity and the highest quality oil generally has the lowest acidity level. Extra virgin oil has the highest grade and is therefore the most expensive. Some of my favourite olive oils are made with the Arbequina olive. These are small olives, green-brown in colour, with a pleasant, peppery flavour and slightly bitter flesh. Their oil has an amazing aroma of green apples, fennel, and freshly cut grass with a hint of almond and citrussy lime. Olive oil should not be exposed to heat, light or air for any length of time. It need not be refrigerated, but should be stored in a cool, dark place. It should be discarded after two years, or at the first sign of turning rancid, so it is best to buy in small amounts and make sure you use it regularly.

MARINATED SALT COD *and* BLACK OLIVE SALAD

Cooking time: N/A
Preparation time: 40 minutes,
plus soaking the salt cod
Serves 4

400g/14oz salt cod (*bacalao*)
1 small red pepper, finely diced
1 small green pepper, finely diced
2 large ripe tomatoes, peeled, quartered
　　and deseeded
15 black olives, pitted
1 tbsp chopped chives
80ml/2½fl oz/⅓ cup olive oil
1 tbsp sherry vinegar
sea salt and freshly ground black pepper

*Esqueixada is occasionally described as the
"Catalan ceviche". You can buy ready-to-cook salt
cod that has already been soaked and de-salted
– alternatively, soak it overnight before cooking.
If salt cod is unavailable, you could substitute
with smoked cod or smoked salmon.*

Unless you are using ready-to-cook salt cod, soak the salt cod in a large bowl of cold water for 24 hours, changing the water 2 or 3 times. Drain the salt cod in a colander and give it a final rinse under running water, then pat dry with paper towels.

Break the salt cod into small pieces and put them into a large serving bowl. Add the diced peppers, tomatoes, black olives, and chopped chives. Pour over the olive oil and vinegar and season to taste. Gently toss, then place in the refrigerator to marinate for at least 30 minutes before serving.

YELLOW GAZPACHO *with* SMOKED SALMON *and* AVOCADO

Cooking time: N/A
Preparation time: 15 minutes, plus marinating and chilling
Serves 4

6 ripe yellow tomatoes
2 cucumbers, peeled, deseeded and chopped
1 large yellow pepper
½ medium white onion, peeled and chopped
2 tbsp sherry vinegar
200ml/7fl oz/scant 1 cup good-quality olive oil
1 garlic clove
300ml/10½fl oz/1¼ cups mango purée
6 ice cubes
sea salt and freshly ground black pepper, to taste

--- **TO SERVE:**
8 slices smoked salmon
1 avocado, peeled and diced

From humble beginnings, gazpacho has gone on to be the most revered and well-travelled chilled soup in the world. It has provided nourishment, quenched thirst and sustained those working in the hot sun for centuries. It even got a mention in Miguel de Cervantes' classic novel Don Quixote *in 1605, and gazpacho has been part of the fabric of Spanish culture ever since. Apparently, Cervantes completed his masterpiece while imprisoned for irregularities in his accounts while working for the government, so he was probably starving at the time and longing for some fresh, tasty food. My yellow gazpacho is a very modern, light and colourful version that the guests at our restaurant adore in the summer months.*

Put all the gazpacho ingredients into a bowl and marinate for at least 30 minutes.

Transfer the marinated mixture to a food processor and blend to a fine consistency. Pass through a fine sieve (strainer) and chill in the refrigerator for at least 2–3 hours.

To serve, place 2 slices of smoked salmon in the middle of each of 4 chilled soup bowls and top each with some diced avocado. Pour over the chilled yellow gazpacho at the table.

GRILLED SEA BREAM *with* CAULIFLOWER PURÉE *and* ANTIBOISE SAUCE

Cooking time: 20–25 minutes
Preparation time: 20 minutes
Serves 2

1 whole sea bream (around
    700–800g/1lb 8oz–1lb 12oz),
    de-scaled and gutted
100ml/3½fl oz/scant ½ cup olive oil
sea salt and freshly ground black
    pepper, to taste

--- **FOR THE ANTIBOISE SAUCE:**
4 tbsp olive oil
4 basil leaves, torn
10 fresh coriander (cilantro) leaves
2 shallots, finely chopped
4 tomatoes, peeled and diced
½ garlic clove, crushed
juice of 1 lemon
sea salt and freshly ground black
    pepper, to taste

--- **FOR THE CAULIFLOWER PURÉE:**
2 tbsp olive oil
1 small cauliflower, trimmed into
    small florets
300ml/10½fl oz/1¼ cups milk
2 salted anchovy fillets
white pepper, to taste

To make the sauce, mix all the ingredients together and set aside for 15 minutes.

Preheat the grill (broiler) to medium.

To make the cauliflower purée, heat the olive oil in a small saucepan over a low-medium heat. Add the cauliflower florets and cook gently until they start to soften, then add the milk. Cook over a gentle heat until the cauliflower is just cooked, about 15–20 minutes. Add the anchovy fillets, then use a hand-held (immersion) blender until it resembles a smooth purée. Add a little white pepper, to taste.

Meanwhile, place the sea bream on a baking sheet and brush with olive oil. Season with salt and pepper, inside and out. Grill (broil) for 6 minutes, then turn and grill the other side until the skin is golden and crisp.

To serve, place the sea bream on a warm serving dish. Spoon over the sauce and serve with the cauliflower purée.

OLIVE OIL-MARINATED STRAWBERRIES *with* PASSION FRUIT *and* LAVENDER CUSTARD

Cooking time: 8–10 minutes
Preparation time: 15 minutes, plus chilling and marinating
Serves 4

400g/14oz fresh strawberries, quartered
100ml/3½fl oz/scant ½ cup olive oil
zest and juice of 1 lime
1 tbsp caster (superfine) sugar
juice and seeds of 1 passion fruit

--- FOR THE LAVENDER AND PASSION FRUIT CUSTARD:
150ml/5fl oz/⅔ cup double (heavy) cream
150ml/5fl oz/⅔ cup milk
1 tsp dried lavender flowers
150ml/5fl oz/⅔ cup orange juice
juice and seeds of 3 passion fruit
6 egg yolks
1 tsp cornflour (cornstarch)
125g/4½oz/scant ⅔ cup caster (superfine) sugar

To make the custard, in a medium saucepan, bring the cream, milk and dried lavender flowers to the boil, then remove from the heat and set aside to infuse for at least 10 minutes.

In a separate small saucepan, bring the orange juice and passion fruit to the boil and reduce to a light syrup, about 2–3 minutes.

In a large bowl, whisk together the egg yolks, cornflour (cornstarch), sugar and passion fruit syrup until smooth, then pour into the cream mixture.

Place the saucepan back over a low heat and cook, stirring continuously, until the mixture just coats the back of a spoon, about 3–4 minutes. Do not boil. As soon as the mixture begins to thicken, remove from the heat. Pass through a fine sieve (strainer) into a bowl, then chill in the refrigerator for at least 2–3 hours.

At least 20 minutes before serving, mix together the strawberries with the remaining ingredients in a large bowl and set aside to marinate.

To serve, half-fill 4 tall glasses with the passion fruit custard, top with the marinated strawberries and serve immediately.

LEMON, ANISE *and* OLIVE OIL MADELEINES

Cooking time: 15 minutes
Preparation time: 15 minutes
Makes about 32 madeleines

100ml/3½fl oz/scant ½ cup olive
    oil, plus extra for greasing
3 eggs
200g/7oz/1 cup caster
    (superfine) sugar
2 lemons: grated zest of 1 and
    juice of 2
12–15 anise seeds, lightly toasted
250g/9oz/scant 2 cups plain
    (all-purpose) flour
1 tsp baking powder
1 pinch salt
icing (confectioners') sugar,
    for dusting

Preheat the oven to
190°C/375°F/gas mark 5. Grease
the madeleine pan/s with a little
olive oil.

In a large bowl, beat together
the eggs, sugar, lemon zest and
anise seeds until foamy, almost
white and doubled in volume (if
you don't have big biceps, use
an electric hand whisk/beater).
Keep whisking and pour in the
lemon juice, then slowly add
the olive oil.

In a separate bowl, sift together
the flour, baking powder and
salt. Using a spatula, gently fold
the flour mixture into the
egg mixture.

Place spoonfuls of the batter
mixture into the prepared
madeleine pan/s and bake for
15 minutes until golden.
Remove from the pans while
still warm and transfer to a wire
rack to cool. Dust with a little
icing (confectioners') sugar
before serving.

Peaches
MELOCOTONES

Nothing beats the succulence of sweet, aromatic
Mediterranean peaches, bursting with flavour.
This juicy, plump fruit provides delicious eating
and can be used in so many different and
interesting ways. They can be poached in sugar
syrup with cinnamon, vanilla and cloves, roasted
with cardamom, or pan-fried and caramelised
with brown sugar and almonds. In drinks, peaches
are perfect partners for Champagne, cassis or
calvados. They also work really well with ginger,
lemons, oranges, strawberries and hazelnuts.
Roast duck is amazingly good with glazed
peaches, and sweet-and-sour peach and saffron
chutney (see page 147) can really liven up cold
meats, pâté and salads during the winter months.

The peach originated in China and was
transported along the silk route to Persia, then
into Europe some 2,000 years ago. Alexander
the Great introduced the peach to Greece and
Rome, where it was known as the queen of fruits.
Peaches grow on deciduous trees belonging to
the rose family and related to the almond. They
stop ripening as soon as they are picked, so it is
important to select firm, ripe fruit with a good
fragrance. Make sure that they are unblemished
and not too hard, and don't buy more than you
plan to use, as fresh peaches are highly perishable
and spoil easily.

SLOW FOOD

"When we lose a flavour, a fragrance, we lose a recipe."
Carlo Petrini

Most of us understand the importance of seasonality, freshness and flavour. Words like "local", "organic" and "artisanal" are everywhere nowadays but it's easy to get lost in marketing jargon and forget exactly what the words mean. That is, until you meet someone like Laura Buades.

Laura is at the forefront of the Slow Food movement* in Spain and her goal is to promote the use of locally produced, seasonal and biodynamic foods. She believes in a reconnection with the lost rhythms of nature and getting back to working the land. Laura believes that processed food is changing the landscape through intensive farming, and also eroding a way of life that revolved around producing and eating great food in a relaxed, sociable way.

As we walked around her garden, she explained how many indigenous fruits and vegetables are under threat from standardisation and commercialisation. "It is overwhelmingly important that we don't lose our forgotten foods. Some of these varieties go back hundreds, or even thousands, of years and are part of our culinary, scientific, genetic and popular cultural heritage; they also ensure our genetic diversity is not lost. Let's eat them, not lose them!"

As Laura handed me the most amazing sun-drenched peach plucked straight from the tree, she went on: "We are what we eat, and the land for future generations will be what we make of it. Together with like-minded farmers, our aim is to raise awareness and protect local, lost varieties, so that they may be rediscovered and returned to the market."

I'm reminded that modern lifestyles and production methods are the main reasons that we are losing so many of our traditional foods. With their demise, we also lose centuries of knowledge and tradition. It is often easier to find food from halfway across the world than food produced on our doorstep. It's time to rebuild the link between our food, the land, and the people who produce it.

* The Slow Food movement was founded by Carlo Petrini and opposes the standardisation of taste, defends the need for consumer information and protects the cultural identities tied to food and gastronomic traditions.

PEACH *and* SAFFRON CHUTNEY

Cooking time: 25–35 minutes
Preparation time: 10 minutes
Makes 4–6 x 500ml/17fl oz jars

200g/7oz tomatoes, deseeded
    and chopped
60g/2oz onion, finely chopped
60g/2oz/½ cup sultanas (golden
    raisins)
200g/7oz/1 cup light brown
    (muscovado) sugar
250ml/9fl oz/1 cup sherry vinegar
1 tbsp sea salt
½ tsp cinnamon
½ tsp ground ginger
½ tsp cayenne pepper
1 large pinch saffron
1kg/2lb 3oz ripe peaches

I love to preserve food in the form of chutney, or compota *as it is known here in Spain. There's a great deal of creative satisfaction to be had in seeing rows of shiny jars filled with really delicious things, stored away ready to enliven all kinds of recipes throughout the rest of the year. It's a great way of not wasting any of the wonderfully fresh, seasonal produce from our farm. I'm a romantic at heart and confess to wanting to keep the great tradition of preserving alive. One of my favourite* compotas *is this slightly spicy peach and saffron chutney. It's the perfect partner for terrines, duck confit, cold meats and, of course, all kinds of cheese.*

Place all the ingredients except the peaches in a heavy saucepan and cook over a low heat, stirring frequently, for 15–20 minutes, until all the ingredients begin to break down.

Meanwhile, blanch the peaches in boiling water for 15 seconds, then refresh them in a bowl of ice-cold water. Peel and cut into large chunks.

Add the peaches to the saucepan with the chutney and cook for a further 10–15 minutes, until the peaches start to break down and the chutney is thick and syrupy.

Pour into sterilised glass jars and let cool, then cover and store in the refrigerator for up to 2 months.

SALAD OF IBERIAN HAM *with* GRILLED PEACHES, HAZELNUTS *and* GOATS' CHEESE DRESSING

Cooking time: 4 minutes
Preparation time: 10 minutes
Serves 4

30g/1oz hazelnuts, peeled
3 fresh peaches, pitted and cut into
    large wedges
olive oil, for brushing
12 slices good-quality Iberian ham
150g/5½oz mixed salad leaves
    (rocket/arugula, lamb's lettuce,
    watercress, etc.)
200g/7oz goats' cheese, crumbled,
    to serve
sea salt and freshly ground black
    pepper

--- FOR THE GOATS' CHEESE
DRESSING:
100g/3½oz soft goats' cheese
1 tsp sherry vinegar
4 tbsp single (light) cream
5 tbsp olive oil
1 tsp Dijon mustard
sea salt and freshly ground black
    pepper

Preheat the oven to
200°C/400°F/gas mark 6.

For the dressing, place all the ingredients in a food processor and blend to a light purée.

Place the hazelnuts on a lipped baking sheet and toast in the hot oven for 2 minutes until golden. Be careful not to burn them – they'll toast very quickly.

Brush the peaches with a little olive oil. Heat a heavy griddle (grill) pan and place the peaches on the grill for 30 seconds on each side, or until grill marks appear. The peaches should be warm but still firm. Remove from the grill and set aside.

Arrange the Iberian ham slices on 4 serving plates. Top with the grilled peaches and salad leaves. Scatter with the toasted hazelnuts and a little crumbled goats' cheese. Serve drizzled with the goats' cheese dressing.

BULGUR *and* PEACH SALAD *with* FETA, POMEGRANATE *and* ZA'ATAR

Cooking time: 15–20 minutes
Preparation time: 15 minutes,
plus chilling
Serves 4

150g/5½oz/scant 1 cup fine bulgur wheat or barley
  couscous
500ml/17fl oz/2 cups water
12 cherry tomatoes, halved
2 tbsp extra virgin olive oil
2 spring onions (scallions), finely chopped
1 tbsp preserved lemons (see page 88), chopped
2 tbsp lemon juice
½ tsp cayenne pepper
1 tsp sea salt
3 tbsp chopped fresh coriander (cilantro)
3 tbsp chopped mint
150g/5½oz feta cheese, crumbled
100g/3½oz/1 cup pomegranate seeds
2 fresh peaches, pitted and quartered
½ tsp za'atar (readymade or see recipe opposite)

--- FOR HOMEMADE ZA'ATAR:
2 tbsp sesame seeds
2 tbsp cumin seeds
2 tbsp finely chopped fresh hyssop (or use fresh thyme
  or oregano)
2 tbsp ground sumac
2 tsp sea salt
1 tsp freshly ground black pepper

Za'atar is an incredibly versatile Middle Eastern spice blend. If you can't find a readymade variety, I have provided a recipe for making your own.

If making your own za'atar, lightly toast the cumin seeds in a dry frying pan (skillet), just until they start to release their aroma and essential oils. Grind to a fine powder in a pestle and mortar, then stir in all the other ingredients. Store in an airtight container for up to 1 month.

Bring the bulgur wheat or barley couscous and water to the boil in a medium saucepan, then reduce the heat and simmer for 12–15 minutes, or until the bulgur wheat is tender. Drain well and chill in the refrigerator for at least 1 hour.

In a large serving bowl, combine the cherry tomatoes, olive oil, spring onions (scallions), preserved lemons, lemon juice, cayenne pepper and salt with the chilled bulgur wheat (barley couscous) and mix well. Stir in the chopped coriander (cilantro) and mint, then sprinkle with the feta cheese, pomegranate seeds, peaches and za'atar.

PEACH AND RASPBERRY SANGRIA

Cooking time: N/A
Preparation time: 5 minutes
Serves 4

2 peaches, pitted and chopped
100g/3½oz/scant 1 cup fresh
    raspberries
juice of 1 lemon
½ tsp ground cinnamon
50ml/2fl oz/¼ cup apricot brandy
200ml/7fl oz/scant 1 cup cava or
    sparkling wine
crushed ice, to serve

Sangria is possibly the ultimate summer thirst-quencher. This red wine punch has become somewhat of a national treasure, but no two sangrias are alike and every Spaniard seems to have a different recipe with completely different ingredients. The classic versions all include red wine, brandy and fresh fruit poured over ice cubes. The cava-producing area of Catalonia has also produced a wonderfully refreshing, sparkling version called zurra, *flavoured with fresh peaches.*

Combine the peaches, raspberries, lemon juice, cinnamon and brandy in a blender or food processor until it resembles a purée. Divide between 4 tall glasses and add crushed ice. Top up with chilled cava or sparling wine and serve immediately.

ROASTED PEACHES *with* LAVENDER CARAMEL *and* CRÈME FRAÎCHE

Cooking time: 20 minutes
Preparation time: 5 minutes
Serves 4

1 tbsp unsalted butter
4 large, ripe peaches, halved and
    pitted
75ml/2½fl oz/⅓ cup clear honey
2–3 sprigs fresh lavender flowers
grated zest of 1 lemon
4 large spoonfuls crème fraîche,
    to serve

Preheat the oven to 200°C/400°F/gas mark 6 and grease an ovenproof baking dish with a little butter.

Arrange the peaches in the baking dish, cut-side up. Drizzle the honey over the peaches and sprinkle over the lavender flowers and lemon zest. Bake for 15 minutes, then remove from the oven and spoon the lavender caramel from the baking dish back over the peaches. Bake for a further 5 minutes, or until the peaches are softened and golden.

Serve immediately, topped with crème fraîche and drizzled with the remaining lavender caramel.

Sun-drenched vegetables hold a very important place in Mediterranean cookery, and I think fresh, shiny peppers with their sweet flavour, crunchy texture and stunning array of colours are the pick of the crop. Peppers begin their lives green and, when left on the stalks to mature, will mellow and begin to turn red, taking on a milder, sweeter flavour. When roasted in the oven with a little olive oil and a couple of crushed garlic cloves, they take on an amazing savoury sweetness. The smell of them cooking is without doubt one of my favourite kitchen aromas.

Peppers feature prominently in so many traditional recipes all over the Mediterranean region, especially here in Spain, where the locals seem to be practically addicted to them. One of the country's most popular dishes found in local tapas bars is simply fried green peppers sprinkled with a little sea salt, called *pimientos de Padrón*. Padrón peppers are named after a tiny village in Galicia and eating them is very much like the food equivalent of Russian roulette, as every now and again there is a chance you'll bite into one unbelievably hot, fiery pepper, capable of bringing tears to your eyes.

TAP DE CORTÍ

In the height of summer, visitors to Mallorca may notice a colourful red pepper – *pebre bord* – being gathered everywhere. These are used to make *tap de cortí*, a type of local paprika. Indigenous to Mallorca, these small red peppers nearly became extinct, but are now being grown in increasingly larger numbers all over the island. In days gone by, the red peppers would be hung from pieces of string known as *enfilalls* to dry out in the sun. Across large parts of the island, the walls of white-washed houses would be covered in these chains of red peppers gently swinging in the afternoon breeze as far as the eye could see. The traditional process to produce *tap de cortí* is a complex one. The peppers are dried in the sun over three to four weeks so that they do not lose their natural antioxidants and thus their capacity to preserve food.

Afterwards, they are put through a stone grinder six times, with a twenty-four-hour break in between for the pimento to cool down. After a sifting process, the paprika is then ready to be packaged. Recently, Mallorca's red pepper has gained official recognition by being entered into the national register for protected trade goods. Having been lost for so many years, Mallorca's little red pepper is now enjoying greater popularity than ever before, and artisan producers are slowly bringing this forgotten treasure back to life.

HOMEMADE HARISSA

Cooking time: 1 minute
Preparation time: 10 minutes
Makes 1 x 350ml/12fl oz jar

2 tsp coriander seeds
2 tsp fennel seeds
2 tsp cumin seeds
1 small red pepper, deseeded
    and chopped
6 large red chillies, deseeded
    and chopped
1 red onion, chopped
4 garlic cloves, crushed
1 tbsp tomato purée (paste)
100ml/3½fl oz/scant ½ cup olive
    oil, plus extra for storage
    if necessary
1 pinch sea salt

This fiery red-hot sauce from North Africa gives a little kick to anything, from stews to marinades and sauces. You can buy it in jars and tubes, but nothing beats homemade harissa, and it really is so simple to make.

Toast the spices in a hot, dry frying pan (skillet) for 1 minute, until fragrant and lightly toasted. Transfer them to a food processor, along with the red pepper, chillies, onion, garlic, tomato purée (paste) and olive oil. Blend to a smooth paste and season with a little salt.

If not using immediately, you can keep the harissa in the refrigerator for up to a week, covered with a layer of olive oil.

RED PEPPER COULIS

Cooking time: 25–35 minutes
Preparation time: 10 minutes
Serves 8–10

2 tbsp olive oil
1 medium onion, chopped
4 red peppers, chopped
2 ripe tomatoes, chopped
2 garlic cloves, crushed
1 sprig fresh thyme
2 bay leaves
300ml/10½fl oz/1¼ cups chicken
    stock (bouillon)
sea salt and freshly ground black
    pepper

This sauce perfectly complements the piquillo peppers stuffed with salt cod brandade (see page 164), but it can also be served with grilled fish, pasta and all types of vegetable dishes. You can substitute the chicken stock (bouillon) with vegetable stock or water, if you prefer. It can be stored for 2–3 days in the refrigerator.

Heat the olive oil in a heavy saucepan over a low-medium heat, add the onion and cook until softened, about 2–3 minutes. Add the red peppers, tomatoes, garlic and thyme, cover with a lid and cook for 5 minutes.

Remove the lid, add the bay leaves and chicken stock (bouillon) and simmer for 20–25 minutes, until the peppers are soft.

Remove and discard the sprig of fresh thyme and the bay leaves. Transfer the mixture to a food processor and blend until smooth. Pass through a fine sieve (strainer) and season to taste.

TUMBET

Cooking time: 20–30 minutes
Preparation time: 15 minutes
Serves 6

200ml/7fl oz/scant 1 cup olive oil
8 potatoes, peeled and sliced
6 garlic cloves, crushed
4 red peppers, deseeded and sliced
  lengthways
2 green peppers, deseeded and
  sliced lengthways
6 aubergines (eggplant), cut into
  thick slices
500ml/17fl oz/2 cups the perfect
  tomato sauce (see page 224)

*This is a classic vegetable dish
from Mallorca consisting
of layers of fried peppers,
aubergines (eggplant) and
potatoes in a rich tomato
sauce. I love to serve it with a
few crispy, grilled lamb cutlets
straight from the barbecue.*

Preheat the oven to
180°C/350°F/gas mark 4.

Heat the oil in a saucepan over
a medium heat, add the potatoes
and fry until golden, about 3–4
minutes. Add 3 of the crushed
garlic cloves and cook for a
further 30–40 seconds. Remove
the potatoes from the pan and
layer them in the bottom of a
large earthenware oven dish.

Meanwhile, add the red and
green peppers to the hot pan
and fry for 3–4 minutes, until
soft. Add the rest of the garlic
and cook for a further 30–40
seconds. Layer the peppers on
top of the potatoes in the dish.

Fry the aubergines (eggplant) in
the same oil for 1–2 minutes on
each side. Layer the aubergines
over the peppers, then pour over
the tomato sauce.

Bake in the oven for 10–15
minutes. Remove from the oven
and serve warm.

MALLORCAN RED PEPPER TART

Cooking time: 40–50 minutes
Preparation time: 20 minutes,
plus proving
Serves 6–8

20g/¾oz/4 tsp fresh yeast (or
10g/⅓oz/1½ sachets active dried
yeast)
150ml/5fl oz/⅔ cup lukewarm
water
300g/10½oz/scant 2¼ cups strong
(bread) flour, plus extra for
dusting
1 pinch paprika
1 tsp sea salt
100ml/3½fl oz/scant ½ cup olive oil

--- **FOR THE TOPPING:**
3 red peppers
2 tbsp olive oil
1 medium onion, diced
3 garlic cloves, thinly sliced
4 salted anchovy fillets, roughly
chopped
10 cherry tomatoes, quartered
sea salt and freshly ground black
pepper

*Mallorca's most popular finger food is coca.
Although the name applies to a wide range of both
sweet and savoury cakes and breads, prepared
and consumed throughout Catalonia, Aragón,
Valencia and all over the Balearic Islands, I
actually prefer the salty, savoury ones. Savoury
cocas exist all over the Mediterranean region,
ranging from Italian pizzas and focaccias, to the
French pissaladière of Provence and the delicious
flatbreads of the Middle East. My favourite coca
is this tart, topped with roasted peppers, tomatoes,
onions and a little salted anchovy. It's the perfect
appetizer to hand out on a hot, sunny day.*

Dissolve the yeast in the lukewarm water.

Place the flour, paprika and salt in a large mixing
bowl and make a well in the middle of the flour.
Slowly pour in the yeast mixture and olive oil,
a little at a time, mixing constantly until fully
incorporated. Knead the dough for 4–5 minutes
until smooth and elastic. Place the dough back in
the bowl, cover with a clean cloth and leave to rise
for about 1½ hours in a warm place, until doubled
in size.

Meanwhile, preheat the oven to 200°C/400°F/gas
mark 6.

Place the red peppers on a baking sheet and roast
in the oven until the skin starts to blacken and
blister, about 15–20 minutes. Transfer the peppers
to a bowl and cover with cling film (plastic wrap).
When cooled slightly, peel off the skin, remove
the seeds and cut the flesh into thick strips.

Reduce the oven temperature to 180°C/350°F/gas
mark 4.

Heat the olive oil in a saucepan over a low heat, add the onion and garlic and gently cook for 3–4 minutes, stirring every now and then. Add the chopped anchovies and cherry tomatoes and remove from the heat, then add the sliced red peppers and season to taste.

Knead the dough on a lightly floured surface, then roll it out to a rectangle about 1cm/½in thick. Place it on a large baking sheet and spread the pepper topping evenly over the dough. Bake for 20–25 minutes until the edges and bottom are golden brown.

Leave to cool before slicing. Serve slightly warm or at room temperature.

ESCALIVADA with GOATS' CHEESE and ANCHOVIES

Cooking time: 35–40 minutes
Preparation time: 15 minutes
Serves 4

2 red onions, unpeeled
150ml/5fl oz/⅔ cup olive oil
2 large aubergines (eggplant)
2 red peppers
2 yellow peppers
2 tbsp lemon juice
2 garlic cloves, crushed
150g/5½oz goats' cheese log, sliced
    into rounds
4 fillets salted anchovies, chopped
sea salt and freshly ground black
    pepper

This is a Catalan speciality of roasted peppers with onions, aubergines (eggplant), garlic and olive oil. The name escalivada comes from the Catalan verb escalivar, "to cook in ashes" – a reference to the traditional preparation of cooking the vegetables over the embers of a wood fire.

Preheat the oven to 200°C/400°F/gas mark 6.

Place the whole, unpeeled onions in a large roasting pan and rub them with a little of the olive oil and some salt. Roast in the oven, turning from time to time, for 15 minutes.

Prick the aubergines (eggplant) in several places with a fork and add them to the roasting pan. Bake the onions and aubergines for 20–25 minutes, until the vegetables are soft but not mushy. Remove from the oven and let them cool slightly.

Meanwhile, roast the peppers in a separate roasting pan for about 20–25 minutes, turning from time to time, until their skins start to blacken and blister. Transfer the peppers to a bowl, cover with cling film (plastic wrap) and set aside to cool slightly.

When cool enough to handle, deseed the peppers, peel the roasted vegetables, and cut them all into thick strips. Combine the sliced vegetables in a large bowl, add the remaining olive oil, lemon juice and the garlic and season with salt and pepper. Transfer to a serving dish and top with the sliced goats' cheese and anchovies.

Serve either at room temperature or chilled, as desired.

PIQUILLO PEPPERS STUFFED *with* SALT COD BRANDADE

Cooking time: 15 minutes
Preparation time: 25 minutes,
plus infusing
Serves 4

20 piquillo peppers, drained and
   tops sliced off
250ml/9fl oz/1 cup (about ½
   quantity) red pepper xoulis
   (see page 158)
olive oil, for greasing

--- FOR THE BRANDADE:
1kg/2lb 3oz salt cod, desalted
   (see page 133)
500ml/17fl oz/2 cups milk
½ onion
2 cloves
2 stalks flat-leaf parsley
500g/1lb 2oz mashed potatoes
150ml/5fl oz/⅔ cup olive oil
3 garlic cloves, crushed
2 pinches nutmeg
1 tsp cayenne pepper
juice of 1 lemon
sea salt and freshly ground black
   pepper

Pimientos del piquillo are red peppers roasted over a wood fire. They have a tangy sweetness and an intense flavour followed by a little kick. Piquillo peppers are often poached slowly in a little olive oil and garlic, then sprinkled with flor de sal and served with grilled meats and fish. However, their triangular shape with a slightly curved point makes them the perfect vehicle for stuffing. You can buy them packed in jars from most supermarkets.

Preheat the oven to 180°C/350°F/gas mark 4 and lightly oil a baking dish with olive oil.

To make the brandade, place the salt cod in a saucepan and cover with the milk. Stud the onion with the cloves and add to the pan along with the parsley stalks and bring slowly to the boil. Remove from the heat and set aside to infuse for 10 minutes.

Remove the salt cod from the milk and place it in a bowl, along with the mashed potatoes. Add the olive oil, garlic, nutmeg, cayenne pepper, lemon juice and 2–3 tablespoons of the infused milk and mix well to form a light purée. Season to taste.

Carefully fill the piquillo peppers with the brandade and place in the oven dish. Pour over the red pepper coulis, cover with a lid or with kitchen foil and bake in the oven for 10 minutes, or until piping hot. Serve immediately.

JOHN DORY *with* STEWED PEPPERS

Cooking time: 20 minutes
Preparation time: 20 minutes
Serves 4

100ml/3½fl oz/scant ½ cup olive oil
1 medium onion, sliced into strips
1 green pepper, deseeded and
    sliced into strips
1 red pepper, deseeded and sliced
    into strips
1 yellow pepper, deseeded and
    sliced into strips
4 tomatoes, chopped
1 garlic clove, crushed
1 tsp paprika
2 tbsp tomato purée (paste)
150ml/5fl oz/⅔ cup dry sherry
200ml/7fl oz/scant 1 cup fish stock
    (bouillon)
4 x 200g/7oz fillets John Dory
2 tbsp chopped flat-leaf parsley
sea salt and freshly ground black
    pepper

Heat most of the olive oil, reserving about 1 tablespoon, in a heavy saucepan over a low-medium heat. Add the onion and peppers and sweat until softened. Add the tomatoes, garlic, paprika, tomato purée (paste), dry sherry and fish stock (bouillon), cover with a lid and cook slowly for about 15 minutes, until the sauce thickens and the vegetables are cooked. Season to taste.

Heat the reserved tablespoon of olive oil in a frying pan (skillet) over a medium heat, add the John Dory fillets, skin-side down, and fry for 2 minutes, until the skin is golden. Carefully turn the fillets over and cook for a further 30 seconds, taking care not to overcook them. Transfer the fillets to the stewed pepper mixture, sprinkle with the chopped parsley and serve immediately.

HAKE *in* a LEMON-CORIANDER CRUST *with* RED PEPPER AIOLI

Cooking time: 30–35 minutes
Preparation time: 20 minutes
Serves 4

4 x 175g/6oz hake fillets, skinned
olive oil, for greasing
green salad, to serve

--- **FOR THE LEMON AND CORIANDER CRUST:**
80g/3oz/1½ cups fresh
    breadcrumbs
40g/1½oz Gruyère cheese, grated
30g/1oz fresh coriander (cilantro)
60g/2oz/½ stick unsalted butter
grated zest and juice of 1 lemon

--- **FOR THE RED PEPPER AIOLI:**
1 red pepper
4 egg yolks
1 tbsp white wine vinegar
2 garlic cloves, crushed
1 tsp English mustard
400ml/14fl oz/1⅔ cups olive oil
sea salt and freshly ground black
    pepper

Preheat the oven to 200°C/400°F/gas mark 6 and lightly oil 2 baking sheets.

Place all the ingredients for the crust in a food processor and blend to a purée. Set aside.

To make the aioli, place the red pepper on a baking sheet and roast in the oven until the skin starts to blacken and blister, about 15–20 minutes. Transfer to a bowl and cover with cling film (plastic wrap). When slightly cooled, peel off the skin, cut in half and remove the seeds.

Add the roasted red pepper, egg yolks, vinegar, garlic, mustard and some salt and pepper to a food processor. Pulse once or twice to blend. With the motor still running, very slowly add the oil in a thin, steady stream. After 1–2 minutes, the mixture will emulsify into a thick, rich sauce.

Cover each hake fillet with a spoonful of the crust mixture and place on a baking sheet. Bake for 15 minutes.

Serve immediately with the red pepper aioli and a green salad.

Red Prawns
GAMBAS ROJAS

Every time I wander around the Olivar market in Palma, I find myself drooling over the stunningly fresh, locally caught red prawns (jumbo shrimp) from Sóller. I don't think it is possible to put anything finer in your mouth, with that intense, wild taste that just explodes when you bite into their juicy firm flesh.

The best way to cook them – *gambas "a la sal"* – is also the easiest. You just scatter a little sea salt over a very hot, flat griddle (grill) and place the whole prawns on top. Let them sit for 20 seconds or so, until they start to toast, then drizzle with a little olive oil. Wait another 20 seconds and scatter them with chopped parsley and crushed garlic. Turn them over, drizzle with a little more olive oil and cook for a final minute. You will be rewarded with an intoxicating aroma and one of the great taste sensations to be found anywhere in the world.

Eating *gambas de Sóller* is not for the timid – you have to get stuck in with your fingers and suck the prawns dry before you begin to wrestle the flesh from its crispy red casing. Some people leave the heads – frankly, this should be made illegal. The juice inside the head is the tastiest part and orgasmically good ... ALL the prawn must be consumed. These prawns are expensive and nothing should go to waste.

The most important thing to look for when buying *gambas de Sóller* is their freshness, which you can tell by the appearance of the shell: they should be a shiny, vibrant red colour, firm to the touch and elastic. If they have been preserved in ice, their head quickly darkens and their gastronomic value is lost. For this reason, it is best to consume them fresh from the sea. If you simply can't handle eating the heads, you should still save them, as they make a wonderful sauce that will add a unique taste to the most humble fish dish.

Most tapas bars serve a dish called *gambas con gabardina* (see page 173), which translates as "prawns in an overcoat". The prawns are shelled, leaving just the top part of the tail attached, then dipped in batter and deep-fried in hot oil until crisp. Another simple, delicious *tapa* is *gambas al ajillo* (see page 175), which can be made in a matter of minutes with garlic, prawns, olive oil and chillies. It normally comes swimming in olive oil, so having some crusty bread on hand to mop up the sauce is imperative.

WHOLE PRAWNS COOKED OVER SALT

Cooking time: 5 minutes
Preparation time: 2 minutes
Serves 2

200g/7oz/1 cup flaky sea salt
10 large red prawns (jumbo
    shrimp), whole in shell
2 tbsp olive oil

Real purists insist on eating prawns "a la sal" with absolutely no accompaniments or frivolous garnishes.

Evenly sprinkle the salt flakes over a heavy frying pan or cast iron skillet and heat over a high heat. When hot, place the whole prawns (shrimp) in a single layer over the salt and cook undisturbed for 2 minutes. Carefully flip the prawns and cook for a further 1 minute on the other side, then sprinkle with a little olive oil.

To eat, gently pull the head from the body and suck the juices from the head. Suck on the shells of the bodies before peeling and eating the tails.

CRISPY FRIED PRAWNS *with* AIOLI

Cooking time: less than 10 minutes
Preparation time: 10 minutes, plus resting
Serves 4–6

2 large eggs
250g/9oz/scant 2 cups plain (all-purpose) flour
1 tsp baking powder
1 pinch salt
1 pinch paprika
250ml/9fl oz/1 cup beer
30 large red prawns (jumbo shrimp), peeled and de-veined, with the tips of the tails left on
vegetable oil, for deep-frying
aioli (see page 55), to serve

In a large bowl, whisk together the eggs, flour, baking powder, salt and paprika. Whisk in the beer, cover with cling film (plastic wrap) and let rest in a warm place for 20 minutes.

Heat enough oil for deep-frying in a deep, heavy saucepan to 190°C/375°F, or until a cube of bread browns in 30 seconds. Dip each prawn (shrimp) into the batter, holding each by the tail, then carefully lower into the oil. Don't overcrowd the pan – work in batches of no more than 5 prawns at a time. Cook for about 1 minute until golden brown. Remove with a slotted spoon to drain on paper towels.

Serve hot with a little aioli for dipping.

OLIVE OIL-FRIED PRAWNS *with* GARLIC *and* CHILLI

Cooking time: 2 minutes
Preparation time: 10 minutes
Serves 4–6

100ml/3½fl oz/scant ½ cup extra
    virgin olive oil
3 large garlic cloves, thinly sliced
1 red chilli, finely chopped
350g/12oz red prawns (jumbo
    shrimp), peeled
2 tbsp chopped flat-leaf parsley
juice of ½ lemon
crusty bread, to serve

Heat the oil in a small frying pan (skillet) over a high heat, add the garlic and chilli and sizzle gently for a few seconds until the garlic takes on a hint of colour, then add the prawns (shrimp). Cook for about 30 seconds, until the prawns are golden on the outside yet still moist inside. Remove from the heat and finish with a sprinkling of parsley and lemon juice. Serve while still sizzling hot, with crusty bread.

CREAMY BOMBA RICE *with* SAFFRON, SEA FENNEL *and* SÓLLER PRAWNS

Cooking time: 25 minutes
Preparation time: 20 minutes,
plus marinating
Serves 4

2 tbsp olive oil
2 shallots, finely chopped
1 garlic clove, crushed
300g/10½oz Bomba rice
½ tsp saffron
30g/1oz fresh sea fennel, finely chopped, plus extra
   few leaves to garnish
1l/35fl oz/4¼ cups fish or shellfish stock (bouillon)
   (made using the heads from the prawns, if possible)
250g/9oz red prawns (jumbo shrimp), peeled
1 tbsp crème fraîche
100g/3½oz Mahón or Cheddar cheese, finely grated
50g/1¾oz/scant ½ stick unsalted butter
1 tbsp chopped chives
sea salt and freshly ground black pepper

--- FOR THE MARINATED FENNEL:
¼ bulb fennel, finely sliced
juice of 1 lemon
2 tbsp extra virgin olive oil
sea salt flakes, to taste

Wild sea fennel, known locally as fenoll marí, grows all around the island's coastal areas and is generally pickled in vinegar and served as a traditional garnish for a classic pa amb oli (bread with tomatoes). It shares flavour characteristics with the fennel herb, specifically a slight anise taste and herbaceous scent.

To make the marinated fennel, place the finely sliced fennel in a bowl, squeeze over the lemon juice and add the olive oil. Season with sea salt flakes, then gently toss everything together and set aside to marinate for 30–40 minutes.

Heat 1 tablespoon of the olive oil in a saucepan over a medium heat, add the shallots and garlic and sweat gently until the shallots start to break down. Stir in the rice, saffron and sea fennel, then add a little hot fish stock (bouillon) until the rice is just covered. Cook, stirring with a wooden spoon, until the liquid has been absorbed. Continue to add the stock gradually, stirring continuously, until all the stock has been absorbed and the rice has softened, about 15 minutes.

Add the red prawns (jumbo shrimp) and cook for a further 1 minute, then stir in the crème fraîche and grated cheese and season to taste. The rice should be light and creamy. Stir in the remaining tablespoon of olive oil, the butter and chives and serve, garnished with the marinated fennel and a few fresh sea fennel leaves.

GRILLED PRAWN SKEWERS *with* SMOKED PAPRIKA *and MOJO VERDE*

Cooking time: less than 5 minutes
Preparation time: 10 minutes,
plus marinating
Serves 4

5 tbsp extra virgin olive oil
1½ tbsp lemon juice
½ garlic clove, finely crushed
1 tsp smoked paprika
450g/1lb red prawns (jumbo
    shrimp), peeled and de-veined,
    with the tips of the tails left on
sea salt and freshly ground black
    pepper
lime wedges, to serve
salad leaves, to serve

--- FOR THE *MOJO VERDE*:
4 garlic cloves
1 small green pepper, deseeded
350ml/12fl oz/scant 1½ cups olive
    oil
100ml/3½fl oz/scant ½ cup sherry
    vinegar
1 tsp ground cumin
1 bunch fresh coriander (cilantro),
    stalks removed
1 pinch sea salt

First, make the *mojo verde*. Place all the ingredients in a food processor and blend to a smooth purée. Store in an airtight container and chill in the refrigerator until required.

In a bowl, combine 2 tablespoons of the olive oil with the lemon juice and the garlic, smoked paprika and some salt and pepper. Add the prawns (shrimp) and marinate for 30 minutes in the refrigerator.

Preheat the grill (broiler) to high or heat a griddle (grill) pan until hot.

Thread the prawns onto small skewers and place on the grill or griddle. Brush with any remaining marinade and grill (broil) for 2–3 minutes until bright pink. Serve with *mojo verde*, lime wedges and green salad leaves.

Rice
ARROZ

Rice, as well as being one of the world's most important crops, is a symbol of life and fertility. At Spanish weddings, it is thrown over the bride and groom. In culinary terms, there are three basic kinds: long, medium and short grain. Long grain is traditionally used in savoury dishes and short grain in dessert cooking. Due to its enormous fame and popularity, you could be forgiven for thinking that Spain's rice dishes start and end with the *paella*. However, the influence of rice on Spanish cookery is undeniable, and many interesting and varied dishes exist throughout Spain and all over the Mediterranean. It is paired with meat, fish, shellfish and vegetables and is widely used to thicken stews and soups.

Valéncia produces virtually all of the rice in Spain, and it has been grown in the Albufera region of Valéncia since the beginning of the nineteenth century. Its production spread north along the Mediterranean coast to the Delta Del Ebro and south into Extramadura and Mallorca. Growing in still water, the rice commonly used for *paella* stretches out for miles in enormous fields. However, each year, a tiny amount of the very best rice in Spain is cultivated in the village of Calasparra in the neighbouring region of Murcia. They grow two historic varieties: Callasparra and the coveted Bomba, which was nearly extinct until gourmet chefs recently recognized its superior qualities. It is cultivated by hand in rice paddies along the banks of the Segura River. At 1,300 feet above sea level, the constant flow of cold, fresh mountain water means that the rice matures more slowly than it would in the still flats along the Valencian shore. It produces a harder grain with less moisture, absorbing one third more broth while retaining its integrity.

The Rolls-Royce of Rice

As a chef, I'm more than a little obsessive about finding the best ingredients for my kitchen. One of the ingredients that I'm obsessing about right now is Acquerello rice. It's organic, aged Italian carnaroli rice. That's right, aged!

Acquerello is grown using a crop rotation system and is the only rice variety sown on the farm, to avoid the possibility of inadvertent hybridisation. After the harvest, the grains of Acquerello carnaroli are aged from one to three years, a process that, by allowing the rice to "breathe", optimises its qualities and characteristics. Ageing renders starch, proteins and vitamins less water-soluble, improving the consistency of the grains and enabling them to absorb more cooking liquid. When cooked, the grains become larger, firmer, do not stick together and taste even better. Acquerello produces 500 tonnes of Carnaroli rice a year

and, while the rice sells for about double the price of other risotto rices, it has become the go-to choice for many of the world's top chefs, including Heston Blumenthal, Thomas Keller and Alain Ducasse, who named it "the Rolls-Royce of rice".

The Art of *Paella*

Spain's most famous dish is also its most contentious one. Opinions vary as to its origins and what constitutes authentic *paella* and exactly what ingredients should be used.

The classic *Paella Valenciana*, like most peasant food, was invented with whatever happened to be at hand. With its rich, fertile soil, Valéncia has an abundance of vegetables growing in the fields. Snails and rabbits would stop by to nibble on the leaves, and these would invariably find their way into the cooking pot too. Add to that the proximity of the Albufera rice fields and the humble beginnings of *paella* were there. It gets its name from the *peallera*, the wide, round cooking dish that it is traditionally served in.

A few years ago, I was lucky enough to receive a masterclass from Rafael Vidal, the king of *paella*. He always makes his paella outside in the open air over a log fire and stands the *paellera* on a tripod over the flames. In his restaurant on the outskirts of Valéncia, he makes huge 50-portion *paellas* and on Sunday lunchtimes he serves up to 500 people. He is a traditionalist and sticks rigidly to the classic, peasant ideals from which *paella* was born. No peppers or fancy seafood for Rafael; his recipe consists of 30 per cent rabbit and 70 per cent chicken, fried in olive oil for 10–15 minutes until they are almost cooked and well toasted. He adds *garrofo* (a type of large broad bean), chopped tomatoes, saffron, sweet paprika and water. He brings this to the boil, adds a large sprig of rosemary, and cooks this for 6–8 minutes. The rosemary is removed and Rafael adds his rice, stirring with a wooden spoon to distribute it evenly. When the old boy judges that the rice is almost cooked, he spreads the fire to reduce the heat and finishes the *paella* slowly over the barely smouldering embers. For more than 40 years, Señor Vidal has remained true to his ideals and changed absolutely nothing. The few hours I spent in his company convinced me of the importance and reverence that this simple, rustic dish has attained in Spanish gastronomy.

The Science Behind the Perfect Risotto

For some strange reason, risotto has a reputation for being difficult and time-consuming to make, when in fact the reverse is true. Making a good risotto takes a little bit of practice, but in essence it's such a simple dish and always a joy to make.

Before you attempt this simple, Italian classic, it's worth understanding just a little science behind the perfect, silky-smooth risotto. Two rules apply: it needs continual stirring with a wooden spoon and the liquid should be hot, full-flavoured and added slowly to help dissolve the starches. Basically, your job is to extract as much starch as possible from every single grain of rice to achieve a delicious, creamy risotto, and you need to create a little friction and steam in the saucepan to achieve that. If you add too much liquid at once, the rice grains are just floating and swimming around in the stock. They need to be in constant contact, rubbing against each other to release all that wonderful starch hidden in the centre of each grain. Risottos are also very sensitive to timing and have to be served immediately to display their rich, creamy texture.

WHITE RISOTTO *with* BEE POLLEN *and* CAPERS

Cooking time: 20 minutes
Preparation time: 10 minutes
Serves 4

1 tbsp olive oil
2 shallots, finely chopped
1 garlic clove, crushed
1 sprig fresh thyme
300g/10½oz risotto rice (preferably Acquerello)
1l/35fl oz/4¼ cups hot vegetable or chicken stock (bouillon)
50g/1¾oz/scant ½ stick unsalted butter
1 tbsp mascarpone
100g/3½oz Parmesan, finely grated
1 tbsp bee pollen
1 tbsp capers
sea salt and freshly ground black pepper

This is a really basic risotto bianco, which can be adapted with the addition of so many different flavours. The caper and pollen combination was originally inspired by Massimiliano Alajmo of Le Calandre restaurant, who serves an incredible white risotto with coffee and capers. I love the balance of the acidic capers with the floral notes of bee pollen.

Heat the olive oil in a heavy saucepan over a medium-low heat, add the shallots, garlic and thyme and gently sweat until the shallots start to break down. Stir through the rice and add enough hot stock (bouillon) to just cover the rice. Cook, stirring continuously with a wooden spoon, until all the liquid has been absorbed. Continue to add the stock gradually, stirring continuously, until all the liquid has been absorbed and the rice has softened, about 15 further minutes. Make sure the risotto is loose and not too thick. Add the butter, mascarpone, grated Parmesan, bee pollen, capers and season to taste. The risotto should be light and creamy. Serve immediately.

"DIRTY RICE" RUSTIC, MALLORCAN-STYLE RICE

Cooking time: 35 minutes
Preparation time: 20 minutes
Serves 6

100ml/3½fl oz/scant ½ cup olive oil
1 onion (preferably Spanish), chopped
4 garlic cloves, crushed
3 tomatoes, peeled and chopped
½ tsp ground cinnamon
1 pinch ground nutmeg
1 tsp paprika
1 large pinch saffron
300g/10½oz mixed wild mushrooms
500g/1lb 2oz rabbit, cut into pieces
3 quails, cut in half
2.5l/85fl oz/scant 11 cups chicken stock (bouillon)
1 x 200g/7oz butifarrón (black pudding), sliced
300g/10½oz Bomba or short grain rice
250g/9oz fresh peas
2 tbsp chopped flat-leaf parsley
sea salt and freshly ground black pepper

*Mallorcan cuisine is very robust and has its roots firmly planted in rustic, peasant fare. One of my favourite recipes is **arroz brut**. Literally translated as "dirty rice" it's a delicious broth cooked in an earthenware pot with rice, rabbit, pork, vegetables and a few snails thrown in for good measure. It's the perfect winter warmer! My recipe is a simple version, with rabbit, quail and butifarrón (a Mallorcan blood sausage or black pudding), but you can substitute with chicken, pork or game when in season. Add a few snails if you want it to be really authentic!*

Heat the olive oil in a heavy saucepan over a medium heat, add the onion and gently cook for about 2 minutes, until softened but not coloured. Stir through the garlic, tomatoes, cinnamon, nutmeg, paprika and saffron and cook for a further 2–3 minutes. Add the wild mushrooms, rabbit, quails and chicken stock (bouillon), bring to the boil, then reduce the heat and simmer for 15 minutes. Add the butifarron, rice and peas and simmer for a further 20 minutes. Use a ladle to skim off any fat and impurities that rise to the surface during cooking.

Season with salt and pepper and add the parsley. Pour into a soup tureen and serve at the table.

SPANISH-STYLE RABBIT *and* SNAIL RICE

Cooking time: 25–35 minutes
Preparation time: 15 minutes
Serves 4

150ml/5fl oz/⅔ cup olive oil

1 x 1.5kg/3lb 5oz whole rabbit, chopped into pieces

24 pre-cooked snails (available online)

2 medium tomatoes, chopped

1 red pepper, deseeded and diced

2 garlic cloves, crushed

1 tsp paprika

350g/12oz Calasparra or Bomba rice

1 pinch fresh saffron

1.2l/40fl oz/5 cups chicken stock (bouillon)

aioli (see page 55), to serve

sea salt and freshly ground black pepper

Heat the olive oil in a wide, heavy frying pan (skillet) or *paella* pan over a medium heat, add the rabbit pieces and fry for about 6–8 minutes, until golden brown. Add the snails, tomatoes, red pepper, garlic and paprika and cook for 3–4 minutes, or until all the liquid has evaporated. Add the rice, saffron and chicken stock (bouillon), season with salt and pepper, bring to the boil and cook for 15–20 minutes, until all the liquid has been absorbed. Remove from the heat and let stand for 2–3 minutes.

Take the whole dish to the table and serve with the rich, garlic aioli.

SLOW FOOD

Long considered a delicacy in Mallorca and beyond, snails have been an integral part of the island's cuisine for centuries, and in most traditional restaurants you'll probably find somebody working their way through a large plateful of them. I know that the thought of cooking and eating snails may seem a forkful too far for some people, but snails have a long and illustrious gastronomic history, having been eaten since Roman times.

Sa Caragolera is a snail farm in the village of Binissalem, where they breed four different types of snails to supply to local restaurants. I have always been told that the best snails are found in vineyards where they feed on the grape leaves, although at Sa Caragolera they are fed on fresh herbs and cabbage.

I occasionally used to eat snails in France years ago – just 6 or 8 snails in a delicious garlic, shallot and herb butter, always nicely presented in a little dish known as an *escargotière*, which ensures a neat presentation with each snail in its own compartment. The first time I ordered them in Mallorca, I couldn't believe it – there must have been at least 50 snails all piled up in an earthenware dish.

They are normally prepared in the following way: first they are soaked in a little salted water with vinegar and flour for about one hour, ridding them of any grit and waste matter. They are then cleaned several times again in fresh water, changing the water every time. The snails are then placed in a saucepan, covered with cold, seasoned water, and slowly brought to the boil over a gentle heat. Any scum or impurities that rise to the surface are removed. Some coarsely chopped onion and red chilli is added, along with a bouquet of fresh herbs containing parsley, thyme, bay leaf and fresh fennel, and they are simmered for about one and a half hours. The snails are then drained and served boiling hot with a garlicky aioli.

Snails are a good option as we look for new sustainable foods. There's not much by-product or waste; you don't have to cut down trees to farm them; they don't eat a lot; plus they are ready to be eaten at six months old. They can also be delicious.

SPANISH-STYLE SEAFOOD RICE

Cooking time: 25 minutes
Preparation time: 20 minutes
Serves 4–6

100ml/3½fl oz/scant ½ cup olive oil
300g/10½oz langoustines
1 medium onion, finely chopped
4 garlic cloves, crushed
400g/14oz short grain rice
1 pinch fresh saffron
1 pinch paprika
2 tomatoes, peeled and chopped
2l/70fl oz/8½ cups fish stock (bouillon)
1kg/2lb 3oz fresh mussels, cleaned and debearded
300g/10½oz fresh clams, cleaned
1 small squid, cleaned and diced
200g/7oz prawns (shrimp), cooked and peeled
300g/10½oz cooked crab meat
sea salt and freshly ground black pepper

Heat the olive oil in a heavy saucepan over a medium heat, add the langoustines and fry until they start to colour. Add the onion and garlic and cook for 1–2 minutes, until the onions start to soften. Stir in the rice, saffron, paprika, tomatoes and fish stock (bouillon) and simmer for about 10 minutes. Add the mussels, clams and squid and continue to simmer until the rice is just cooked, about 10 minutes. Add the cooked prawns and crab meat, season to taste and serve.

CUTTLEFISH RICE

Cooking time: 25–30 minutes
Preparation time: 20 minutes
Serves 6

100ml/3½fl oz/scant ½ cup olive oil
1 medium onion, finely chopped
1 green pepper, finely chopped
2 large garlic cloves, finely
    chopped
2 tomatoes, peeled and chopped
1 tsp paprika
500g/1lb 2oz cuttlefish or squid,
    cleaned and diced
1l/35fl oz/4¼ cups fish stock
    (bouillon)
4 squid ink sachets
400g/14oz Bomba or short grain
    rice
sea salt and freshly ground black
    pepper
lemon wedges, to serve

This rice dish is great served on its own, but is delicious served topped with a piece of freshly grilled fish and some aioli (see page 55). All Spanish supermarkets stock frozen squid ink sachets. If you have trouble finding them, ask your friendly fishmonger for 3-4 fresh ink sacs from the cuttlefish or squid.

Heat the olive oil in a wide frying pan (skillet) or a *paellera* (*paella* dish) over a low-medium heat. Add the onions, green pepper and garlic and sweat for about 2 minutes, until softened. Add the chopped tomatoes, paprika and cuttlefish or squid and gently cook for another 6–8 minutes. Add the fish stock (bouillon) and ink sachets and bring to the boil. Season with salt and pepper, then add the rice. Simmer for about 12–15 minutes, until the rice is cooked and all the liquid has been absorbed. Remove from the heat and let rest for 3–4 minutes before serving with wedges of lemon alongside.

ACQUERELLO RICE *with* LANGOUSTINES, ASPARAGUS *and* BURRATA

Cooking time: 25–30 minutes
Preparation time: 10 minutes
Serves 4

20 asparagus tips
2 tbsp olive oil
2 shallots, finely chopped
1 garlic clove, crushed
250g/9oz Acquerello rice
100ml/3½fl oz/scant ½ cup white wine
800ml/28fl oz/scant 3½ cups hot fish stock (bouillon)
20 langoustine tails, peeled
150g/5½oz Parmesan, grated
50g/1¾oz/scant ½ stick unsalted butter
1 x 400g/14oz burrata cheese
sea salt and freshly ground black pepper

This has to be the ultimate risotto! Acquerello rice, sweet langoustines, fresh, crisp asparagus spears and creamy burrata. Burrata takes mozzarella to another level; super creamy and utterly delicious. It's a type of mozzarella that is formed into a pouch and then filled with soft, stringy curd and cream.

Blanch the asparagus tips in boiling water for about 3–4 minutes. Drain and set aside.

Heat 1 tablespoon of the olive oil in a heavy pan over a low heat, add the shallots and garlic and gently sweat for about 1–2 minutes until they start to break down. Increase the heat to medium, add the rice and wine and stir until the wine has been absorbed. Add enough hot fish stock (bouillon) to just cover the rice and continue to stir until all the liquid has been absorbed. Continue to add the stock gradually, stirring continuously, until all the liquid has been absorbed and the rice has softened, about 15–20 further minutes. Add the langoustine tails and grated Parmesan and season to taste. The rice should be light and creamy. Remove from the heat and stir in the butter.

Meanwhile, heat the remaining olive oil in a small frying pan (skillet) and warm the asparagus tips through.

To serve, divide the rice and asparagus tips between 4 warmed bowls and top with pieces of creamy burrata. Serve immediately.

Saffron
AZAFRAN

These bright red stamens have been highly prized since ancient times, when they were used to perfume bathing water and as a dye – everything it touches turns yellow. The word "saffron" comes from the Arabic *za'faran*, meaning golden. It is said to have anaesthetic properties and has also been used as a remedy for sleeplessness and to reduce the effects of a hangover. It's also supposed to be a good aphrodisiac and put you in a happy mood.

Spanish saffron has been grown in La Mancha for at least 1,000 years, and the region is now world-famous for producing the planet's most expensive spice. If you consider that 85,000 flowers are needed to obtain just one kilo of saffron, it's hardly surprising that it's so expensive. Until recently, we had to import our saffron for the restaurant from the mainland, but that changed when the Mallorcan company Especias Crespí embarked on a new challenge to expand and diversify its offerings. In 2016, they planted 20,000 saffron crocus plants in the village of Vilafranca. This is only the beginning, as they plan to plant up to 200,000 more. Their goal is to produce up to 25 kilos of saffron per year, and the production will be entirely ecological.

The Spanish make liberal use of saffron and it is used to flavour and colour many of their most famous rice dishes, including *paella*. It has an unusual, slightly bitter, earthy taste and gives food a faint aroma and an intense yellow colour. It appears in fish soups and stews throughout the Mediterranean and works really well with fresh mussels, scallops, red mullet and Dover sole.

Being expensive, it is obviously best used sparingly, but a little does go a long way. Try to buy fresh, good-quality saffron and avoid the powdered variety if at all possible. If you put a little into a pestle and mortar and add a tiny amount of warm stock (bouillon) or water, you can pound the saffron to intensify the taste and colour before using.

SAFFRON-CRUSTED BAKED COD *with* PEA *and* LEMONGRASS SOUP

Cooking time: 25 minutes
Preparation time: 15 minutes
Serves 4

olive oil, for greasing
4 x 200g/7oz thick cod fillets
100g/3½oz/¾ cup pine nuts
1 yellow pepper, deseeded
    and chopped
1 garlic clove
2 tbsp olive oil
1 large pinch saffron
sea salt and freshly ground black
    pepper

--- **FOR THE PEA AND LEMONGRASS SOUP:**
50g/1¾oz/scant ½ stick butter
3 small leeks, finely chopped
2 sticks lemongrass, finely
    chopped
1 onion, finely chopped
2 potatoes, peeled and diced
1.5l/52fl oz/6½ cups chicken stock
    (bouillon)
1kg/2lb 3oz fresh peas, shelled
250ml/9fl oz/1 cup milk
sea salt and freshly ground black
    pepper

Preheat the oven to 220°C/
425°F/gas mark 7 and grease
a baking sheet with olive oil.

To make the soup, heat the
butter in a pan over a medium
heat, add the leeks, lemongrass
and onion and sauté until
softened but not coloured, about
2–3 minutes. Add the potatoes
and stock (bouillon) and bring
to the boil. Cook, covered, for 15
minutes, then add the peas and
cook for 5 minutes more. Add
the milk, season to taste and set
aside to cool a little. Blend until
smooth, then sieve (strain).

Meanwhile, place the cod fillets
on the baking sheet and season
with salt. Put the pine nuts,
yellow pepper, garlic, olive oil
and saffron into a food processor
and blend to a thick paste. Pat
the mixture over the cod fillets,
pressing to make it stick. Bake
in the middle of the oven for 6–8
minutes, until the fish is opaque.

To serve, place the cod fillets,
crust-side up, in 4 warmed soup
bowls and pour the soup around.

WHITE BEANS *with* FRESH CLAMS *and* SAFFRON

Cooking time: 40–50 minutes
Preparation time: 15 minutes
Serves 4

200g/7oz dried white beans
    (cannellini or butter beans)
2 bay leaves
1 sprig fresh thyme
3 garlic cloves, peeled
100ml/3½fl oz/scant ½ cup olive oil
1 large onion, finely chopped
1kg/2lb 3oz fresh clams, cleaned
400ml/14fl oz/1⅔ cups fish stock
    (bouillon)
1 tsp saffron
2 tbsp fresh breadcrumbs
2 tbsp chopped parsley
sea salt and freshly ground black
    pepper

Fabada is a classic, heart-warming stew from Asturias, traditionally served with white beans (faves), pork and chorizo. Along the coastline, they prepare a simpler version with fresh clams and saffron that is absolutely delicious!

Place the white beans, bay leaves, thyme and 1 garlic clove in a large saucepan, cover with cold water and bring to the boil. Reduce the heat, cover with a lid and simmer for 30–40 minutes, until the beans are tender.

In a separate saucepan, heat the olive oil over a low-medium heat, add the onions and cook until they start to soften, about 2 minutes. Add the fresh clams and fish stock (bouillon) and bring to the boil. Cook for 2–3 minutes until the clams have opened (discard any that remain closed). Pour the cooked clams and stock into the pan with the cooked beans.

In a pestle and mortar, crush the remaining garlic cloves with the saffron and breadcrumbs to form a paste. Remove the beans from the heat and stir in the breadcrumb mixture and the chopped parsley. Season to taste and serve immediately.

MALLORCAN-STYLE SEA BASS *with* A SAFFRON *and* OLIVE OIL PARMENTIER

Cooking time: 20 minutes
Preparation time: 20 minutes
Serves 4

4 x 150g/5½oz sea bass fillets
olive oil, for frying
baby spinach leaves, to garnish
sea salt and freshly ground black
    pepper

--- FOR THE VINAIGRETTE:
50ml/2fl oz/¼ cup sherry vinegar
30g/1oz/3 tbsp sultanas (golden
    raisins)
200ml/7fl oz/scant 1 cup olive oil
200g/7oz cherry tomatoes, halved
2 tbsp pine nuts, lightly toasted
2 tbsp chopped flat-leaf parsley

--- FOR THE SAFFRON AND OLIVE
OIL PARMENTIER:
250g/9oz potatoes, peeled
1 small onion, chopped
1 large pinch saffron
800ml/28fl oz/scant 3½ cups fish
    stock (bouillon)
200ml/7fl oz/scant 1 cup olive oil
juice of 1 lime

Sea bass 'a la Mallorquina' is one of my favourite dishes. The textures, colours and freshness really define Mediterranean cookery at its very best. The traditional version is a whole fish baked over sliced potatoes and spinach. I've given the dish a very modern twist while retaining the essence and flavours of this wonderful recipe.

To make the vinaigrette, bring the sherry vinegar to the boil in a small saucepan. Add the sultanas (golden raisins) and remove from the heat. Leave to cool until the sultanas have soaked up all the vinegar and are plump. Mix in the olive oil, cherry tomatoes, pine nuts and chopped parsley. Season to taste and set aside.

To make the saffron and olive oil parmentier, combine the potatoes, onions, saffron and fish stock (bouillon) in a saucepan and bring to the boil. Simmer for 15 minutes, until the potatoes are just cooked, then remove from the heat and add the olive

oil and lime juice. Transfer to a food processor and blend to a purée. Pass through a fine sieve (strainer), season to taste and keep warm.

Preheat the oven to 220°C/425°F/gas mark 7.

Season the sea bass fillets with salt and pepper. Heat a little olive oil in a heavy, oven-proof frying pan (skillet) over a medium heat, add the fillets, skin-side down, and cook for 1–2 minutes until the skin becomes crisp and golden. Turn over and cook for a further 1 minute. Transfer the pan to the oven for about 2 minutes to finish cooking.

To serve, place the sea bass fillets in the middle of 4 large soup bowls. Spoon over a large spoonful of the vinaigrette and pour a little warm saffron and olive oil parmentier around the outside. Serve immediately, garnished with the baby spinach leaves.

SAFFRON-SPICED CAULIFLOWER COUSCOUS *with* RED PEPPER CHERMOULA

Cooking time: 8–10 minutes
Preparation time: 15 minutes
Serves 4

½ cauliflower
80g/3oz/scant ½ cup couscous
200g/7oz canned cooked chickpeas
    (garbanzo beans), drained and rinsed
1 pinch saffron
½ tsp ground cumin
½ tsp ground coriander
¼ tsp cayenne pepper
1 pinch ground cinnamon
150ml vegetable stock (bouillon)
2 tbsp sultanas (golden raisins)
2 tbsp coarsely chopped fresh coriander (cilantro)
sea salt and freshly ground black pepper

--- **FOR THE RED PEPPER CHERMOULA:**
2 canned red peppers, drained
1 garlic clove, crushed
½ tsp harissa paste
3 tbsp chopped fresh coriander (cilantro)
1 tsp ground cumin
1 tsp paprika
juice of 1 lemon
sea salt and freshly ground black pepper

To make the red pepper chermoula, place all the ingredients in a food processor and blend until smooth.

Finely grate or pulse the cauliflower in a food processor until it resembles couscous. Be careful not to over-mix – you don't want to purée the cauliflower. In a large bowl, mix the cauliflower with the couscous, chickpeas (garbanzo beans), saffron, cumin, ground coriander, cayenne pepper and cinnamon.

In a small saucepan, bring the vegetable stock (bouillon) to the boil and pour over the couscous. Cover tightly with clingfilm (plastic wrap) and let stand for 6–8 minutes, until the couscous is just cooked. Add the sultanas (golden raisins) and chopped coriander (cilantro) and lightly mix with a fork to combine. Season to taste and serve with the red pepper chermoula.

SAFFRON, RASPBERRY *and* ORANGE BLOSSOM *CREMA CATALANA*

Cooking time: 40–45 minutes
Preparation time: 15 minutes,
plus standing and chilling
Serves 4

500ml/17fl oz/2 cups milk
150ml/5fl oz/⅔ cup single (light)
    cream
1 large pinch saffron
1 vanilla pod, split
grated zest of 1 orange
2–3 drops orange blossom syrup
6 egg yolks
90g/3¼oz/scant ½ cup caster
    (superfine) sugar
20 fresh raspberries, plus extra
    to garnish

Saffron, fresh raspberries and orange blossom are prefect additions to Crema Catalana. The creams are traditionally thickened over a low heat, but I prefer to bake mine slowly in the oven to limit the risk of the eggs curdling. The creams should have a slight wobble when removed from the oven.

Preheat the oven to 90°C/200°F/gas mark ¼.

In a heavy saucepan, heat the milk, cream, saffron, vanilla pod and orange zest and bring slowly to the boil. Remove from the heat and leave to infuse for 15–20 minutes. Add the orange blossom syrup and strain through a fine sieve (strainer).

In a separate bowl, whisk together the egg yolks and sugar, then stir in the cream mixture until combined.

Pour the mixture into earthenware or ramekin moulds and place 5 raspberries into each mould. Bake for about 35–40 minutes until just set. Do not be tempted to turn the oven temperature up, as they will curdle. Remove from the oven, then chill in the refrigerator for at least 2–3 hours.

To serve, sprinkle with sugar and caramelise under a hot grill (broiler) or with a culinary blowtorch. Garnish with fresh raspberries and serve immediately.

Squid

CALAMAR

Every time I pick up an octopus or a squid, I can't help thinking that something so ugly couldn't possibly taste so good. But looks can often be deceiving, and these creepy-looking cephalopods are utterly delicious when cooked in the right way. For me, nothing beats super-fresh whole squid grilled over a fierce flame and sprinkled with garlic, parsley, olive oil and sea salt. The tentacle adventure needn't be all that scary – just remember that there is one basic rule when cooking with cephalopods: they either need to be cooked quickly for a very short time, or slowly for a very long time; anything in between and you end up with something rather tough and unpleasant.

Some nations still seem to be a little nervous about things with tentacles, especially the British. Until fairly recently, British fishermen would throw squid and cuttlefish back into the sea! The Spanish have never been so squeamish or choosy, and cephalopods are enormously popular throughout the country. There are many authentic squid (*calamar*), cuttlefish (*sepia*) and octopus (*pulpo*) recipes to be found, although fried squid (*Calamares a la Romana*) is probably the country's favourite *tapa*.

Octopus means "eight feet" and it's these feet, or tentacles, along with the lower body, that are the delicacy of this somewhat unusual-looking cephalopod. They are delicious just boiled for 40–45 minutes, sliced and drizzled with olive oil and sprinkled with paprika and sea salt.

A few years ago, I was extremely pleased to be invited out along the Cantabrian coast to fish for squid. What I hadn't bargained for is that squid fishing is a nocturnal activity and that we were going to set sea in a rather tiny rowing boat. Luckily I don't suffer from seasickness, but as we rowed out to sea I must admit that I felt more than a little queasy and almost panic-stricken about the size of the waves. Squid are surface-swimmers, almost transparent and therefore invisible to predators. The fishermen shine lights onto the water to attract the squid and cast out a thin line armed with tiny hooks every 20cm/8in, which is dragged along the surface to ensnare the squid. As they reeled the line back in, it was amazing to see the squid shooting ink and dramatically changing colours.

Hand-fishing with hook and line is painstaking and requires much patience, but the quality of the squid is substantially better than that of net-caught squid. A net-caught squid will have been bashed and crushed and will have sand inside its skin and body. You have to wash net-caught squid thoroughly and completely remove the skin, which takes away both flavour and colour. In local Spanish fish markets you should look out for *Calamar de potera*, which means the squid are line-caught and therefore of a much higher quality. Obviously they are a little more expensive, but they are well worth it.

Preparing fresh squid or cuttlefish is really a simple process, and once you've done it a couple of times, it becomes child's play. Pull the head and tentacles away from the body, then skin the body and pull out the plastic-looking backbone cartilage. Cut the tentacles from the head just above the eye, then wash both the body and tentacles thoroughly in cold running water.

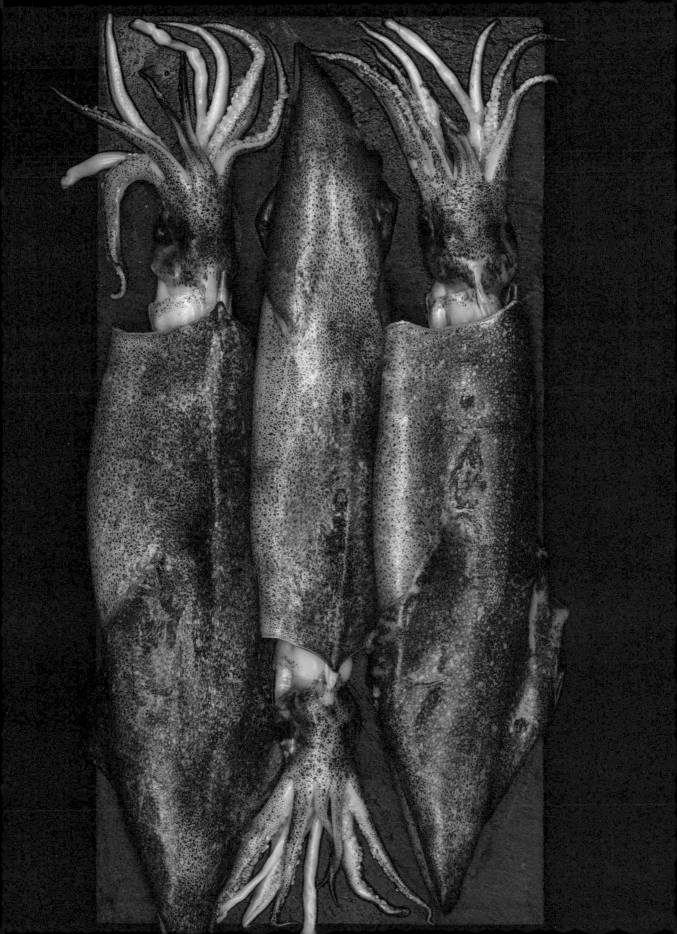

SALAD OF SQUID, NEW POTATOES, CHORIZO *and* ROCKET *with* PASSION-FRUIT OIL

Cooking time: 8–10 minutes
Preparation time: 25 minutes
Serves 4

16 new potatoes, boiled and halved
olive oil, for drizzling
2 squid, cleaned and cut into large
    squares
16 thin slices Ibérico chorizo
2 bunches rocket (arugula)
sea salt and freshly ground black
    pepper

--- **FOR THE PASSION-FRUIT OIL:**
pulp of 4 passion fruit
150ml/5fl oz/⅔ cup orange juice
150ml/5fl oz/⅔ cup olive oil
sea salt and freshly ground black
    pepper

To make the passion-fruit oil, bring the passion fruit pulp and orange juice to the boil in a small saucepan, then reduce the heat and gently simmer for about 2–3 minutes, until the mixture just starts to thicken. Pass through a fine sieve (strainer) into a bowl. Whisk in the olive oil, season to taste and set aside.

In a separate bowl, toss the potatoes in a drizzle of olive oil and season to taste.

Heat a griddle (grill) pan over a high heat. Place the potatoes on the pan and sear for 1–2 minutes, then transfer to a large bowl. Sear the squid pieces for 30 seconds on each side, then transfer to the bowl. Finally, add the chorizo slices to the pan to warm through, then transfer to the bowl. Add 2 tablespoons of the passion-fruit oil to the warm ingredients in the bowl, then add the rocket (arugula) and mix well.

Serve, drizzled with a little more passion-fruit oil.

GRILLED SQUID *with* CHICKPEA, PIQUILLO PEPPER *and* PRESERVED LEMON SALAD

Cooking time: 2 minutes
Preparation time: 20 minutes, plus
1–2 hours chilling
Serves 4

2 medium squid, cleaned and
    sliced into large pieces
olive oil, to drizzle
1 red chilli, finely chopped
8 mint leaves, chopped
sea salt and freshly ground black
    pepper

--- **FOR THE SALAD:**
12 piquillo peppers from a jar,
    sliced
200g/7oz/1½ cups cooked canned
    chickpeas (garbanzo beans)
2 tbsp chopped mint leaves
2 tbsp capers, rinsed
1 tsp preserved lemon (see page
    88), finely chopped
2 garlic cloves, crushed
4 tbsp extra virgin olive oil
juice of 1 lemon
1 large pinch paprika (preferably
    Mallorcan Tap de Corti)
sea salt, to taste

*Chickpeas (garbanzo beans), piquillo peppers and preserved lemons are a great combination and work so well with the fresh squid, mint and chillies. Delicious and a real crowd-pleaser! I use a local paprika called **Tap de Corti**, but you can substitute any type of sweet or slightly smoked paprika, if desired.*

To make the salad, combine all the ingredients in a large bowl and refrigerate for 1–2 hours to let the flavours mingle.

When ready to serve, heat a griddle or frying pan (skillet) until very hot. Season the pieces of squid and place them in the hot pan, along with a drizzle of olive oil. Cook for 30 seconds, until slightly caramelised. Turn the squid over, add another drizzle of olive oil and spinkle with the chopped chilli and mint. Cook for 1 minute, then remove to a serving plate. Serve immediately with the chilled salad.

SPICY FRIED CALAMARI *with* SQUID-INK AIOLI

Cooking time: 5 minutes
Preparation time: 25 minutes
Serves 4

20g/⅔ oz/scant ¼ cup cornflour
    (cornstarch)
50g/1¾oz/generous ⅓ cup plain
    (all-purpose) flour
1 tsp cayenne pepper
½ tsp smoked paprika
350g/12oz squid, cleaned and cut
    into 1cm/½in rings, tentacles
    left whole (or halved if large)
vegetable oil, for deep-frying
lemon wedges, to serve
sea salt and freshly ground black
    pepper

--- **FOR THE SQUID-INK AIOLI:**
4 tbsp aioli (see page 55)
1 sachet squid ink

To make the squid-ink aioli, whisk the aioli and squid ink together in a small bowl and refrigerate until required.

Combine the flours, cayenne pepper and paprika in a bowl and season well. Add the squid rings and tentacles to the flour mixture and toss to coat thoroughly. Place the squid in a sieve (strainer) and shake any excess coating back into the bowl.

Heat enough oil for deep-frying in a deep, heavy saucepan to 190°C/375°F, or until a cube of bread browns in 30 seconds. Deep-fry the squid for 2–3 minutes, or until golden and crisp, turning halfway. Remove with a slotted spoon to drain on paper towels.

Serve immediately, sprinkled with a pinch of sea salt flakes, with the squid-ink aioli and lemon wedges.

MOROCCAN-SPICED OCTOPUS *and* POTATO STEW

Cooking time: 55 minutes
Preparation time: 25 minutes
Serves 4

150ml/5fl oz/⅔ cup olive oil
1 onion (preferably Spanish),
    finely chopped
1 red pepper, diced
2 garlic cloves, crushed
350g/12oz octopus, cleaned
    and cut into 4cm/1½in pieces
1 tsp paprika
1 tsp cayenne pepper
2 tsp ras el hanout (see page 97)
1 cinnamon stick
1.5l/52fl oz/6½ cups vegetable
    stock (bouillon)
400g/14oz tomatoes, chopped
400g/14oz potatoes, peeled, halved
    lengthways and cut into thick
    slices
2 tbsp chopped flat-leaf parsley
2 tbsp chopped fresh coriander
    (cilantro)
crusty bread, to serve
sea salt and freshly ground black
    pepper

Heat the olive oil in a large, heavy saucepan over a low–medium heat, add the onions, peppers and garlic and cook until the onions start to soften. Add the octopus, paprika, cayenne pepper, ras el hanout and cinnamon stick, cover with the vegetable stock (bouillon) and chopped tomatoes and simmer gently for about 30 minutes.

Add the sliced potatoes and continue to simmer for about 20 minutes, until the potatoes are just cooked. Use a ladle to skim off any fat or impurities that rise to the surface during cooking.

Season the stew with salt and pepper, sprinkle with chopped parsley and coriander (cilantro) and serve with crusty bread.

CUTTLEFISH
PICA-PICA

Cooking time: 25–40 minutes
Preparation time: 20 minutes
Serves 4

1–1½ tbsp olive oil
2 onions (preferably Spanish),
    finely chopped
600g/1lb 5oz cuttlefish, cleaned
    and diced
2 garlic cloves, crushed
1 small red chilli, finely chopped
2 tbsp dry white wine
2 tbsp tomato purée (paste)
200g/7oz fresh tomatoes, peeled
    and chopped
2 tbsp finely chopped flat-leaf
    parsley
sea salt and freshly ground black
    pepper

Pica-pica means "hot and spicy". A simple and delicious cuttlefish recipe from Mallorca, this is normally served as part of a tapas spread, but I love it as a snack with crusty bread and olive oil. Cuttlefish is the underrated relation of squid and it has a slightly meatier texture and sweeter flavour. Unless you know exactly what you are doing, ask your local fishmonger to clean the cuttlefish, as it is packed with ink and can get very messy!

Heat the olive oil in a heavy saucepan over a low heat, add the onions and sweat until softened but not coloured. Add the cuttlefish, garlic, chilli and wine and cook for 3–4 minutes, until all the wine has evaporated. Add the tomato purée (paste) and chopped tomatoes and season to taste. Cook for a further 20–30 minutes, until the cuttlefish is tender. Sprinkle with chopped parsley and serve immediately.

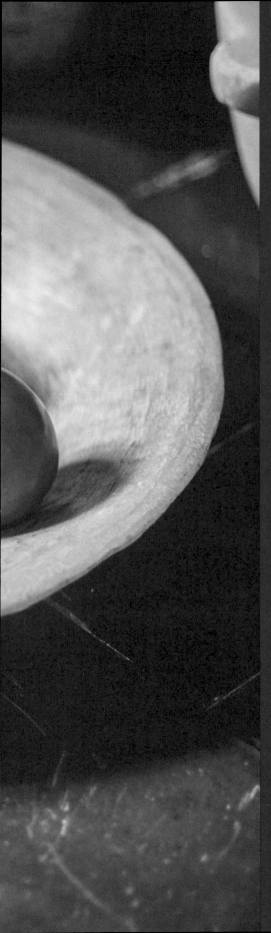

Tomatoes
TOMATES

Juicy, vine-ripened tomatoes are the ultimate Mediterranean summer ingredient. Full of flavour, with a slightly aromatic scent, they are one of those magical ingredients that seem to make others sing. The Spanish love tomatoes so much, they celebrate them with the traditional *Tomatina Fiesta*. Every year on the last Wednesday in August, the town of Buñol in Valencia prepares to get seriously messy when it stages what has become the world's biggest food fight, during which about 150 tons of tomatoes are thrown at party-goers with abandon.

With such a tomato culture, it's no surprise that Spanish growers produce some of the tastiest varieties in the world. For something different, try to find beefsteak tomatoes, known here as *cor de bou* (beef hearts). Some regard them as the "*pata negra*" of tomatoes and it's hard to disagree. Unlike other varieties, the ripening process occurs from the inside out. So the best time to buy them is when the tomatoes begin to display orange streaks on the green skin. As they mature, the reddish streaks on the green skin become a deeper red. The flavour is equally delicious, but you will sacrifice some of the crisp texture. Although normally sold at a premium price, tomatoes still attached to the vine are well worth the extra expense. It is the stem that gives the distinctive aroma, rather than the fruits themselves, but they can be picked when they are very ripe and generally have a better flavour.

All that glitters is not gold, and good looks are often deceptive when buying tomatoes. If you can, pick them up and smell them – chances are, if they smell of nothing, they will probably taste of nothing. Never store tomatoes in the fridge as this impairs the natural ripening and flavour; instead, store them at room temperature. Over-ripe tomatoes will deteriorate even more quickly if chilled.

MEDITERRANEAN UMAMI: UNLOCKING THE FIFTH TASTE

Umami is the enigmatic fifth taste – a rich, meaty flavour and a catalyst that unlocks and defines the deliciousness in certain savoury foods. About 3,000 years ago, Greek philosophers came up with the concept of our four elemental tastes: sweet, salty, sour and bitter. Their theory remained intact right up until the early twentieth century, when a scientist in Japan discovered a fifth, slightly more complicated taste: umami. In Japan, people traditionally used *dashi* – an umami-rich stock made from *kombu* (seaweed) – to illicit the best flavour from food, so the concept of umami has been recognised in the East for a long time. Obsessive chefs now believe that if you can find the perfect balance of the five basic tastes (sweet, salt, bitter, sour *and* umami), you'll have some sort of culinary utopia!

Thankfully, for those who don't want to douse all their food in soy or fish sauce, there are some naturally occurring umami-rich foods, such as sardines, mackerel, oysters, mushrooms, truffles, soy beans, potatoes and tomatoes.

Tomatoes take on a particularly intense umami flavour when they are dried. There are a number of reasons why the flavour of tomatoes changes during both the cooking and drying processes, largely to do with the introduction of fairly high levels of salt to help remove moisture. During cooking, this causes the flavour molecules to become more concentrated, intensifying the resulting flavour. Without getting too technical, over the course of the tomato drying process, the glutamic acid in the tomatoes breaks down even further and changes into different aroma molecules. A basic tomato sauce or ketchup will have lots of umami, but when you dry tomatoes, they have considerably more. Try making your own sun-dried tomatoes (see page 225) and unlock all that hidden umami!

THE PERFECT
TOMATO SAUCE

Cooking time: 40–45 minutes
Preparation time: 10 minutes
Serves 8

100ml/3½fl oz/scant ½ cup olive oil
1 large red onion, finely chopped
3 garlic cloves, crushed
1kg/2lb 3oz beefsteak tomatoes
    (preferably *cor de bou*), peeled,
    deseeded and chopped
1 tbsp sugar
2 tbsp sherry vinegar
4 basil leaves, torn
2 bay leaves
1 sprig fresh thyme
sea salt and freshly ground black
    pepper

A well-made tomato sauce is the cornerstone of so many classic Mediterranean dishes, and it's really simple and satisfying recipe to make. I use cor de bou tomatoes, but you can also use beefsteak tomatoes or plum tomatoes, when in season. Don't be afraid to use canned tomatoes if you can't find full-flavoured, sun-ripened varieties.

Heat the olive oil in a heavy saucepan over a low-medium heat, add the onion and garlic and sweat until they just start to break down, about 3–4 minutes. Add the chopped tomatoes and cook for 5 minutes, stirring from time to time. Add the sugar, vinegar and herbs and cook slowly for 30–35 minutes, until the sauce has reduced and thickened. I like my tomato sauce to be thick, with a really intense flavour, but if you prefer it a little thinner, just add a little water during cooking.

Pass through a fine sieve (strainer) and season to taste. Pour into sterilised air-tight containers and refrigerate for up to 1 week or freeze for up to 3 months.

SUN-DRIED TOMATO PESTO

Cooking time: N/A
Preparation time: 10 minutes
Makes about 300g/10½oz

2 garlic cloves, peeled
150g/5½oz sun-dried tomatoes (see page 226 to make your own)
1 tbsp pine nuts
2 tbsp freshly grated Parmesan
freshly ground black pepper, to taste
100ml/3½fl oz/scant ½ cup olive oil

Pesto rosso is a variation on traditional green pesto. The addition of sun-dried tomatoes gives it a distinctive, milder flavour. Try it with pasta, smeared on bruschetta or brush it over a chicken before roasting.

Place all the ingredients except the oil into a food processor and blend on a high speed, gradually adding the oil through the feed tube, until well combined. Store the pesto in a tightly sealed sterilised jar in the refrigerator for up to 2 weeks.

HOMEMADE SUN-DRIED TOMATO KETCHUP

Cooking time: 20–30 minutes
Preparation time: 20 minutes
Makes about 450–500ml/15½–17fl oz/1¾–2 cups

2 tbsp olive oil
1 red onion, chopped
3 garlic cloves
2cm/¾in piece of root ginger, peeled and chopped
1 red chilli, deseeded and chopped
4 fresh tomatoes, deseeded and chopped
2 tbsp tomato purée (paste)
250g/9oz sun-dried tomatoes (see page 226 to make your own), chopped
1 tbsp brown (turbinado) sugar
2 tbsp red wine vinegar
1 tsp paprika
300ml/10½fl oz/1¼ cups cold water
sea salt and freshly ground black pepper

Heat the olive oil in a large, heavy saucepan over a low heat, add the onion, garlic, ginger and chilli and gently cook for 5–6 minutes until softened, stirring occasionally. Add the fresh tomatoes, tomato purée (paste), sun-dried tomatoes, sugar, vinegar, paprika and cold water, bring to the boil, then reduce the heat and simmer gently for 15 minutes.

Blend the mixture in a food processor until smooth, adding a little more water if necessary. Season with salt and pepper and pass through a fine sieve (strainer). Keep the ketchup in a sterilised airtight container in the refrigerator for up to 3 weeks.

OVEN "SUN-DRIED" TOMATOES

Cooking time: 6–8 hours
Preparation time: 20 minutes,
plus standing
Makes about 800g/1lb 12oz

2kg/4lb 7oz ripe plum tomatoes
1 tbsp sea salt (preferably *flor de sal*)
6 garlic cloves, crushed
4 tbsp chopped oregano
2 tbsp chopped rosemary
freshly ground black pepper, to taste
extra virgin olive oil, for drizzling

Almost an indispensible ingredient in my kitchen, sun-dried tomatoes add a really tasty kick to so many Mediterranean recipes.

Preheat the oven to the lowest heat setting (110°C/225°F/gas mark ¼ or lower if possible).

Slice the plum tomatoes in half horizontally and scoop out most of the seeds. Salt the insides and place them, cut-side down, on a wire cooling rack for 30 minutes. Rinse off the salt under running water and pat dry.

Mix the garlic with the oregano, rosemary and some black pepper and sprinkle the mixture over the cut sides of the tomatoes. Place the tomatoes, cut-side up, on a wire rack over a roasting pan and drizzle with olive oil. Place in the oven for 6–8 hours, until thoroughly dried out.

Pack the dried tomatoes into a large sterilised jar and cover with olive oil. Store in a cool, dark place for no longer than 6 months. Refrigerate on opening and keep for 1 month, topping up the olive oil if necessary.

HERB-ROASTED *COR DE BOU* TOMATOES

Cooking time: 25–30 minutes
Preparation time: 10 minutes
Serves 4

4 beefsteak tomatoes (preferably
   cor de bou)
25 basil leaves
12 sprigs thyme
olive oil, for drizzling
1 bunch chives, chopped
sea salt and freshly ground black
   pepper

These "meaty" tomatoes are just perfect for roasting, but any large beefsteak tomato will suffice.

Preheat the oven to 180°C/350°F/gas mark 4.

Remove the stalk from the tomatoes to create a small cavity and cut 2 slashes on each side. Push most of the basil leaves (reserve a few for garnish) and all of the thyme sprigs into the cavities and the slashes.

Place the tomatoes on a baking sheet, drizzle with olive oil and sprinkle generously with salt and pepper. Bake for 25–30 minutes, until the tomatoes are cooked and lightly caramelised.

To serve, carefully place the tomatoes in a serving bowl and drizzle with the cooking juices from the pan and some fresh olive oil. Garnish with chopped chives and fresh basil leaves.

CHILLED TOMATO *and* PIQUILLO PEPPER SOUP *with* FRESH BASIL

Cooking time: 30 minutes
Preparation time: 20 minutes, plus chilling
Serves 4

800g/1lb 12oz ripe tomatoes, chopped
10 piquillo peppers
1 red onion, chopped
3 garlic cloves, peeled and crushed
4 tbsp good olive oil, plus extra for serving
200ml/7fl oz/scant 1 cup mineral water
few drops Tabasco sauce (optional)
1 handful basil leaves
sea salt and freshly ground black pepper

Roasting the tomatoes for this soup really intensifies the flavour and it could also be served hot, if you prefer. The piquillo peppers can also be be substituted with two deseeded and chopped red bell peppers.

Preheat the oven to 200°C/400°F/gas mark 6.

Put the tomatoes, piquillo peppers, onion and garlic onto a lipped baking sheet, sprinkle with salt and pepper and drizzle generously with olive oil. Mix with your hands to ensure everything is well combined and bake for about 30 minutes, turning occasionally, until the vegetables are tender and just slightly charred.

Blend the roasted vegetables along with the mineral water in a food processor until smooth, then pass through a fine sieve (strainer). Check the seasoning and add the Tabasco if you need a little kick. Chill in the refrigerator for at least 3 hours or overnight.

To serve, ladle into soup bowls, scatter with fresh basil leaves and drizzle with a few drops of olive oil. Serve immediately.

TOMATO, OREGANO *and* BLACK OLIVE TART

Cooking time: 25–30 minutes
Preparation time: 15 minutes
Serves 4

300g/10½oz readymade shortcrust pastry
12 cherry tomatoes, halved
16 black olives, pitted
20 fresh oregano leaves
4 eggs
350ml/12fl oz/1½ cups double (heavy) cream
100g/3½oz Parmesan, grated
sea salt and freshly ground black pepper
rocket (arugula) leaves, to serve

Preheat the oven to 180°C/350°F/gas mark 4.

Line a 20cm/8in tart pan with the shortcrust pastry, cover with greaseproof (wax) paper and fill with baking beans (pie weights). Bake for 10 minutes, then remove the baking beans and greaseproof paper and bake for a further 3–4 minutes, until the pastry is crisp.

Place the chopped tomatoes in a sieve (strainer) and drain well to remove all the excess juice. Spread the tomatoes over the pastry case and sprinkle with the black olives and oregano leaves.

Beat the eggs with the cream and season to taste. Pour over the tomatoes and bake the tart for a further 10–15 minutes, until just set.

Meanwhile, preheat the grill (broiler) to high.

Sprinkle the tart with the grated Parmesan and grill (broil) until golden brown. Leave to cool and serve warm with a rocket (arugula) salad.

"*MORO TRAMPÓ*" SALAD

Cooking time: N/A
Preparation time: 20 minutes, plus standing
Serves 4

4 very ripe vine-ripened tomatoes, peeled and finely diced
2 long green peppers, deseeded and finely diced
2 red chillies, deseeded and finely diced
1 small cucumber, peeled, deseeded and finely diced
½ small onion, peeled and finely diced
2 tbsp finely chopped flat-leaf parsley
½ tsp pomegranate molasses
1 tsp sherry vinegar
3 tbsp extra virgin olive oil
few fresh mint leaves, torn
sea salt and freshly ground black pepper

On hot summer days, a simple tomato salad is hard to beat. Trampó is the perfect dish to enjoy for lunch on a warm day in Mallorca. Simply made with tomato, green pepper and onion and dressed with salt and olive oil, the name trampó comes from trempar or "to dress" in Mallorquí. The basic recipe is often spruced up with the addition of anything from artichokes, capers, olives, potatoes and boiled eggs to chickpeas, tuna or salted cod. For my version of trampò, I'm giving it a little Middle Eastern flavour with the addition of pomegranate molasses, red chilli and mint.

Place the tomatoes, peppers, chillies, cucumber and onion in a salad bowl. Add the parsley, pomegranate molasses, sherry vinegar and the extra virgin olive oil and stir so that everything is very well combined. Set aside to macerate for 20 minutes.

Season with salt and pepper, scatter with torn mint leaves and serve immediately.

CHERRY TOMATO, POMEGRANATE *and* FETA SALAD

Cooking time: N/A
Preparation time: 10 minutes
Serves 6

450g/1lb mixed cherry tomatoes,
    halved
1 small red onion, very finely sliced
1 tbsp red wine vinegar
1 tbsp pomegranate molasses
1 tsp honey
3 tbsp extra virgin olive oil
4 tbsp pomegranate seeds
150g/5½oz feta cheese, crumbled
10 fresh mint leaves
sea salt and freshly ground black
    pepper

This is a classic combination, and it doesn't get any better! A mixture of colours for the cherry tomatoes looks really nice.

Place the cherry tomatoes in a bowl and add the red onion, vinegar, pomegranate molasses, honey and olive oil. Season to taste and mix well.

Transfer to a serving dish and sprinkle with the pomegranate seeds, feta cheese and fresh mint leaves. Serve immediately.

Truffles and Wild Mushrooms
TRUFAS Y SETAS

Some years ago, my obsession with truffles caused a bit of a stir on an airplane. I had travelled to France in search of buried treasure, to meet a man who had dedicated his whole life to the pursuit of fresh truffles. After meeting the man and his dog, I carefully inspected the black beauties and handed over a king's ransom for twenty-four amazing, aromatic, fresh truffles. I had spent so much money there was no way I was going to let them out of my sight, so I packed them neatly into my hand luggage and headed back to the airport. It was a very cold afternoon and I was confident that no one would notice the hidden treasure in my bag. I managed to get through security without a problem, but ten minutes into our flight, when the heating really started to kick in, a slight smell started wafting around the cabin. Pretty soon, the whole plane was filled with the heavy aroma that Gareth Renowden once described in *The Truffle Book* as resembling "old socks and sex"! After the cabin crew received several complaints from other passengers, I had no choice but to hold my hand up and confess that it was the contents of my hand luggage that was causing offence... some people don't appreciate a culinary jewel when they smell one. These days, I'm happy to say that I don't need to travel too far for my truffles, as I have another guy with a dog who hunts them in the mountains of Mallorca.

There are many different varieties of truffle, but the most pocket-friendly are summer truffles (*Tuber aestivum*) that come into season from April to September. They have a rough black exterior and brown flesh mottled with white veins. Summer truffles have a delicate but distinctive aroma and are ideal for canapés, pasta sauces, eggs, potatoes, rice or meat and fish dishes. Black winter truffles (*Tuber melanosporum*) are available from November to March and have a distinctive and powerful aroma. You can find white truffles from November to February, and they have a golden exterior with delicate cream-coloured flesh and a strong, musky, slightly garlicky aroma. They are almost never cooked but are usually consumed fresh, typically by being shaved into paper-thin slices over pasta, risotto or salad.

If you buy fresh truffles, store them in the fridge and use within a week. A lot of cooks choose to preserve truffles in uncooked rice grains. The rice grains protect the natural moisture in the truffles, while preventing them from getting too damp. The truffles, in turn, add their amazing flavour to the rice, which will produce a decadent, heavenly, creamy risotto.

Just as there's something special about truffles, so too wild mushrooms. The fact that they have defied modern cultivation methods and only grow wild in woodlands and meadows adds to their mystery. Wild mushroom varieties have been gathered since 3500BC. The Greeks exported them to the Romans, who considered them food for the gods.

Although autumn (fall) is traditionally considered the best season for wild mushrooms, Spain's varied microclimate helps to offer a steady supply all year round. In Mallorca, a local variety called *esclata-sangs* (which translates as "blood mushrooms") is extremely popular when they come into season. They are large, robust-flavoured, meaty fungi that are just perfect for grilling (broiling) or roasting.

You can use any large field mushrooms, but the best way to cook them is to sprinkle them with a little sea salt, a good drizzle of olive oil, add a couple of crushed garlic cloves and plenty of freshly chopped parsley before placing them under a hot grill (broiler) for 5–6 minutes. You'll need some crusty bread to soak up all those delicious cooking juices and, be warned, the aroma can be very addictive.

PAPPARDELLE *with* LOBSTER, TRUFFLE *and* CHIVES

Cooking time: 10–12 minutes
(depending on pasta)
Preparation time: 10 minutes
Serves 4

300g/10½oz pappardelle pasta
1 x 750g/1lb 10oz cooked lobster
50g/1¾oz/scant ½ stick unsalted
    butter
1 tbsp olive oil
2 garlic cloves, crushed
250ml/9fl oz/1 cup double (heavy)
    cream
1 tsp tomato purée (paste)
2 tbsp chopped chives
200g/7oz Parmesan, freshly
    grated
1 black truffle (optional)
sea salt and freshly ground black
    pepper

It really doesn't get any more decadent or more delicious than lobster and truffle! You can substitute the pappardelle for almost any kind of fresh pasta.

Bring a large saucepan of salted water to the boil and cook the pappardelle pasta until *al dente* (check the instructions on your packet for cooking time).

Meanwhile, cut the lobster in half and crack the claws open. Remove the meat from the shell and cut into chunks.

Heat the butter and olive oil in a large saucepan over a low-medium heat, add the garlic, then stir in the cream and the tomato purée (paste). Simmer for about 2 minutes, until reduced and thickened.

Drain the cooked pasta and add to the sauce along with the lobster meat, tossing to coat in the sauce. Season to taste with salt and pepper, then transfer to a serving bowl and scatter over the chopped chives and freshly grated Parmesan. Finally, grate over the black truffle to taste and serve immediately.

BLACK TRUFFLE, SAGE *and* PECORINO RISOTTO

Cooking time: 20 minutes
Preparation time: 10 minutes
Serves 4–6

900ml/31fl oz/scant 4 cups
    chicken stock (bouillon)
30g/1oz/¼ stick butter
1 onion, finely chopped
2 garlic cloves, crushed
350g/12oz arborio or carnaroli
    risotto rice
1 tsp chopped sage leaves
100ml/3½fl oz/scant ½ cup
    dry white wine
1 tbsp mascarpone
1 tsp truffle oil
2 tbsp grated Pecorino cheese
1½ tsp olive oil
fresh black truffle, for shaving
    (optional)
sea salt and freshly ground black
    pepper

In a small saucepan, bring the chicken stock (bouillon) to a simmer.

In a separate heavy saucepan over a medium heat, heat the butter until melted, then add the onion and garlic and cook for about 2 minutes, stirring, until the onion has softened. Stir in the rice and sage leaves, then add the wine and cook, stirring, until fully absorbed. Add enough of the hot chicken stock to just cover the rice. Continue to stir until the rice has absorbed all the liquid. Continue to add the stock gradually, stirring continuously, until all the stock has been absorbed and the rice has softened, about 15 further minutes.

Add the mascarpone, truffle oil and grated Pecorino and season to taste. The risotto should be light and creamy. Stir in the olive oil and serve immediately, topped with freshly grated truffle, if desired.

CELERIAC, TRUFFLE, SMOKED BACON *and* THYME SOUP

Cooking time: 35 minutes
Preparation time: 20 minutes
Serves 6

2 tbsp olive oil
1 onion, finely chopped
50g/1¾oz smoked bacon, cut into
    small pieces
1 leek, white only, finely chopped
2 garlic cloves, crushed
2 sprigs thyme, leaves picked
700g/1lb 9oz celeriac (celery root),
    peeled and diced
800ml/28fl oz/scant 3½ cups
    chicken stock (bouillon)
200ml/7fl oz/scant 1 cup double
    (heavy) cream
2 tsp chopped chives
sea salt and white pepper
fresh truffle slices or a few drops
    of truffle oil, to garnish

The great French chef Auguste Escoffier said, "Soup puts the heart at ease, calms down the violence of hunger, eliminates the tension of the day, and awakens and refines the appetite." Beethoven claimed that "only the pure of heart can make good soup". One thing is for sure – freshly made soups rarely get the attention they deserve, but this delicious one, with celeriac (celery root), smoked bacon, thyme and truffles, leaves everyone wanting more!

Heat the olive oil in a large saucepan over a low-medium heat, add the onion, bacon and leek and cook, stirring occasionally, for 2–3 minutes, until softened but not coloured. Add the garlic and thyme and cook for another 30 seconds, then add the celeriac (celery root) and stock (bouillon) and bring to the boil. Reduce the heat to low, cover and simmer for 30 minutes.

Remove the pan from the heat and let cool slightly. Add the cream and then blend to a smooth purée with a hand-held (immersion) blender or in a food processor. Season to taste with salt and white pepper, then pass through a fine sieve (strainer).

Ladle into soup bowls, scatter with chopped chives and sliced truffle or drizzle with a few drops of truffle oil. Serve immediately.

FRESH CHICKEN STOCK (BOUILLON)

For most of us, soup represents nourishment, healing and comfort, and the secret to good soup is to make the perfect stock (bouillon). Stocks need a little care and attention but, if you follow these basic rules, you'll be rewarded with clear-looking, healthy broths with flavours that are true and clean. Remember, if you make fresh stocks, you can also freeze them to use later.

For a simple chicken stock, place 2 clean chicken carcasses in a large saucepan and cover with cold water. Bring slowly to the boil and use a slotted spoon to skim off fat and impurities from the surface as they rise to the top. Reduce the heat to a gentle simmer, then add 2 small diced onions, 2 crushed garlic cloves, 2 sliced carrots, 1 chopped leek, 1 bay leaf, 1 celery stick and 2 sprigs of fresh thyme. Cook slowly for 2–3 hours, adding a little extra cold water from time to time and continuing to skim the surface when necessary. Finally, pass through a fine sieve (strainer) and your stock is ready to use.

ROSEMARY-ROASTED MUSHROOMS *with* GARLIC-ANCHOVY BUTTER

Cooking time: 15–20 minutes
Preparation time: 15 minutes,
plus 30 minutes chilling
Serves 6

500g/1lb 2oz flat mushrooms,
   cleaned and halved
1 tbsp finely chopped rosemary
   leaves
1 small red chilli, deseeded and
   finely chopped
3 tbsp olive oil
1 tbsp balsamic vinegar
chopped flat-leaf parsley, to
   garnish
sea salt and freshly ground black
   pepper

--- **FOR THE GARLIC-ANCHOVY
BUTTER:**
250g/9oz/2¼ sticks unsalted
   butter, softened to room
   temperature
4 salted anchovy fillets in oil,
   drained and chopped
2 garlic cloves, crushed
2 tbsp chopped flat-leaf parsley
grated zest of 1 lemon
sea salt and freshly ground black
   pepper, to taste

For the garlic-anchovy butter, put all the ingedients into a bowl and mix until well combined. Scrape the butter mixture out onto a sheet of cling film (plastic wrap) or baking parchment and roll into a cylinder shape. Chill in the refrigerator for at least 30 minutes until firm.

Preheat the oven to 200°C/400°F/gas mark 6.

Arrange the mushrooms in a roasting pan in a single layer. Sprinkle with the rosemary, chilli, olive oil and balsamic vinegar and add 4 or 5 thin slices of the garlic-anchovy butter. Bake in the oven for 15–20 minutes, until tender.

Scatter with a little chopped parsley, season and serve immediately.

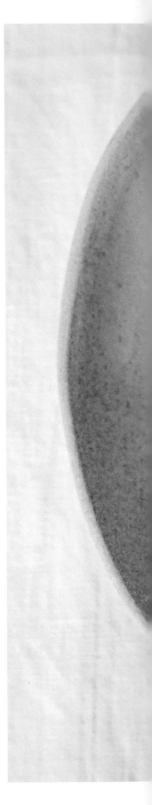

ARTICHOKES *with* WILD MUSHROOMS, TRUFFLE *and* SERRANO HAM

Cooking time: 30 minutes
Preparation time: 10–20 minutes
Serves 4

4 tbsp olive oil
1 medium onion, finely chopped
3 garlic cloves, crushed
200g/7oz mixed wild mushrooms,
    cleaned and chopped
80g/3oz Serrano ham, diced
1 tbsp plain (all-purpose) flour
120ml/4fl oz/½ cup dry sherry
    or white wine
150ml/5fl oz/⅔ cup vegetable stock
    (bouillon)
juice of 1 lemon
8 thin slices fresh truffle (optional)
2 tbsp chopped chives
sea salt and freshly ground black
    pepper

--- FOR THE ARTICHOKES:
8 globe artichokes
juice of 1 lemon
sea salt and freshly ground black
    pepper

Artichokes are incredibly versatile, and they make awesome partners for truffle, mushrooms and Serrano ham. If you don't want to prepare the artichokes, you could also use good-quality artichokes from a jar.

To prepare the whole artichokes for poaching, pull off the lower, outer and discoloured leaves and trim the stems to form a flat base so that the artichokes will stand upright. Cut off about a quarter to one-third of the artichoke leaves straight across the top. Rub the cut surfaces with a little lemon juice to prevent browning. Stand the artichokes on their flat bases in a non-reactive saucepan, add water to a depth of about 5cm/2in, add the lemon juice and season with salt and pepper. Cover and gently simmer for 15–20 minutes. Once cooked, quarter the artichokes and scoop out and discard the hairy chokes with a spoon. Set aside.

Heat the olive oil in a large frying pan (skillet) over a medium heat, add the onion and garlic and sauté until softened, about 2–3 minutes. Add the wild mushrooms and Serrano ham and cook for 1–2 minutes, then add the flour and stir well. Stir in the dry sherry or wine and vegetable stock (bouillon) and cook for about 2 minutes, until the sauce thickens. Add the artichoke quarters and lemon juice and warm through, then scatter with the truffle slices and chopped chives. Season to taste and serve immediately.

INDEX

ACKNOWLEDGMENTS

PICTURE CREDITS

I would like to extend my gratitude to everyone involved the production of this book. I have to start by thanking my awesome wife, Iris, for her tireless work and generally putting up with me everyday in everything we do!

None of this would have been possible without Nando "one-shot" Esteva. Thank you for your friendship and for bringing my food to life with your stunning photography.

I'm also eternally grateful to Barbara Levy for not giving up and helping to make this book become a reality, and to my wonderful restaurant team (especially Luigi & Ignacio), thank you for your support, enthusiasm and dedication.

Many thanks also to Emily Preece-Morrison for the help in writing and editing, and, last but not least, a very special thanks to Daniel Hurst, Georgina Hewitt and all the team at Watkins publishing for your guidance, patience and understanding!